SCALE ELEMENTS
for design elevations

SCALE ELEMENTS
for design elevations

Richard M. McGarry
Greg Madsen

VNR VAN NOSTRAND REINHOLD
New York

🌳 THE SURREY INSTITUTE OF ART & DESIGN

Farnham Campus, Falkner Road, Farnham, Surrey GU9 7DS

The quotation on page 146 from *Landscaping with Container Plants* by Jim Wilson: Copyright© 1990 by Jim Wilson. Reprinted by permission of Houghton Mifflin Co.

I(T)P   Van Nostrand Reinhold is an International Thomson Publishing company.
        ITP logo is a trademark under license.

Manufactured in the United States of America

Van Nostrand Reinhold
115 Fifth Avenue
New York, NY 10003

International Thomson Publishing GmbH
Konigswinterer Str. 518
5300 Bonn 3
Germany

International Thomson Publishing
Berkshire House,168-173
High Holborn, London WC1V 7AA
England

International Thomson Publishing Asia
38 Kim Tian Rd., #0105
Kim Tian Plaza
Singapore 0316

Thomas Nelson Australia
102 Dodds Street
South Melbourne 3205
Victoria, Australia

International Thomson Publishing Japan
Kyowa Building, 3F
2-2-1 Hirakawacho
Chiyada-Ku, Tokyo 102
Japan

Nelson Canada
1120 Birchmount Road
Scarborough, Ontario
M1K 5G4, Canada

16 15 14 13 12 11 10 9 8 7 6 5 4 3

Library of Congress Cataloging-in-Publication Data
McGarry, Richard M., 1948-
     Scale elements for design elevations / Richard McGarry, Greg Madsen.
        p.   cm.
     Includes index.
     ISBN 0-442-00694-2
     1. Entourage (Architectural rendering) 2. Measured drawing.
I. Madsen, Greg. II. Title.
NA2780.M37   1991
720'.28'4—dc20   90-26613

Contents

Acknowledgments

A number of friends and fellow professionals helped us develop the material for this book. Wendy Lochner, senior editor at Van Nostrand Reinhold, championed our idea, refined the text, and navigated the project through the myriad details of production. The Litzman family, of Photo Arts of Miami, did all the camera work in preparing the drawings for publication. Elvis Cruz, of the City of Miami Fire Department, provided fire and rescue equipment details. Captain Henry D. Moorman, of American Airlines, consulted on airplane selection, and both Boeing Corporation and Bell Helicopter provided data on their products.

Tom Pope and Ed McIntyre inadvertently provided the initial inspiration for this book during a visit to their architectural office in Key West, Florida.

And a special thanks to Stephen Nevitt and Leslie Mayberry for their support and encouragement.

Introduction

Like most designers, you probably have lots of great ideas. But graphically communicating them to your clients—and potential clients—with style and pizazz can sometimes be a problem.

This book was created to help you make one specific type of graphic communication, your elevations, into a better design sales tool to use with your client.

Just stripping away the web of dimension lines and specification notes from working-drawing elevations and adding a splash of color is not enough to transform them into an effective design presentation. The key elements of human scale and activity, entourage, and implied depth and light are necessary to make your design elevations "come alive" for your client.

The following pages provide you with over 1700 ready-to-trace, scaled entourage elements for elevations, plus plenty of techniques and short-cuts for using them to display your design concepts in the best possible context.

We sincerely hope this book will help you make more of your great ideas into the three-dimensional realities of the future.

Richard M. McGarry & Greg Madsen

*T*he future, it could be
argued, is the true medium
of the designer.

Paul Stevenson Oles
Drawing The Future

Techniques For Using Entourage

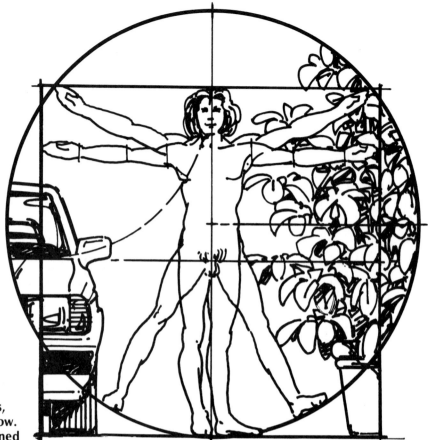

Designers create the buildings, products, and tools of tomorrow. But the future has to be explained in terms of its relationship to the present-day to be clearly understood.

Is your concept bigger than a breadbox? Larger than your client's desk? Can a person walk under it or step over it? You can answer these questions by adding dimension lines and notes to your drawing, but they don't create the instant scale recognition and interest that just sketching in a few entourage elements can.

The ancient philosopher Pythagoras observed that "man is the measure of all things," and the placement of a human figure next to an object is always the best way to show its relative size. But familiar vehicles and foliage can also provide effective scale and ambience for a design presentation. The entourage that you wrap around your presentation elevations is a simple way to give your clients a firm grip on how your new design relates to their known world.

BEYOND SCALE

Entourage can also show information on the intended usage of your design and the kind of people that might use it. For example, look at the elevation of an object shown below. How much can you comprehend about the design, other than that it has a rectangular shape and a deep groove near the top?

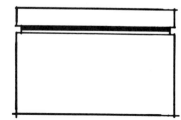

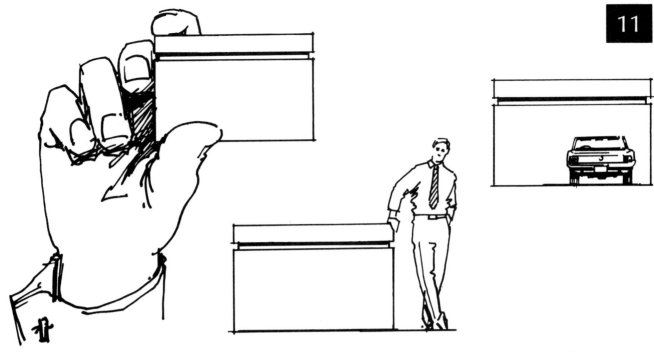

Now consider several different drawings of the same elevation, each identical to the first one, except for a single added piece of entourage.

Notice how much you can now presume about both the size and character of the object being portrayed. The structure behind the jet airliner seems to become a hangar, for example, while the man seems to be leaning on a countertop, and the hand appears to be holding the kind of small gift box used for jewelry.

Entourage can tell a story about the character of a design in a number of ways:

- Palm trees and people in shorts imply a tropical climate; while snow and a mountain backdrop set the scene for a ski resort drawing.

- A cluster of people headed for the entrance of a retail store suggests a successful, profit-making business.

- A luxury car in front of a residence can make the design appear more upscale, whereas children playing on the sidewalk and a station wagon in the driveway signifies a family-oriented neighborhood.

- A person reaching for, looking at, or pointing to an important design element will help focus viewer attention on it.

- The level of dress, from T-shirt casual to black-tie formal, can help explain what kind of people the design is intended for.

- A preponderance of senior citizens, women, teenagers, or uniformed employees, for example, can subtly change the message your picture conveys.

- Foliage or a cluster of people can obscure a part of your design that you want to de-emphasize.

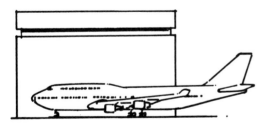

USING THE MATERIAL

All the drawings in this book can be photocopied, then cut and pasted on an elevation, and the whole montage photocopied again to create a finished presentation elevation. Or the drawings can be copied onto clear, adhesive plastic film and stuck into position on your drawing for diazo reproduction.

If you are working with a CAD system and have a scanner, you can take advantage of the fastest, easiest solution of all: scan the material you need, store the digitized version in your image bank, and drop it into your drawings as needed. Computer technology also makes it simple to reposition the entourage drawings; a series of variation studies of different entourage combinations takes just a few minutes.

The slowest, but perhaps most expressive, way to add the drawings to your elevations is to trace them into place. The act of hand-tracing the material allows you to integrate it with your individual drawing style, and often generates a more creative, dramatic presentation.

Whenever possible, use the drawings only as a starting point. Try to interpret them in your personal drawing "language." Drop the details you don't want, add shade and shadow to fit the mood of the rest of your picture, and let the signature traits of your own drawing hand take over.

Numerous variations can be created by tracing only the outline of the material, for example, or dropping the outline and shading in a silhouette. The entourage could be handled as a scribble "gesture" drawing, or rendered with straightened, architectural lines and crossed corners. The drawing could be done only in a dashed outline, or created as a light shape in a dark background. The possibilities are limited only by your imagination.

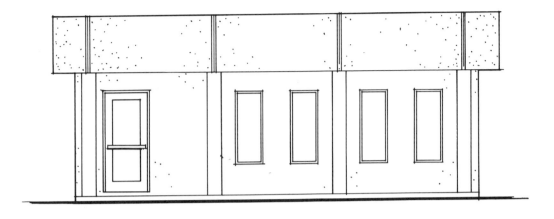

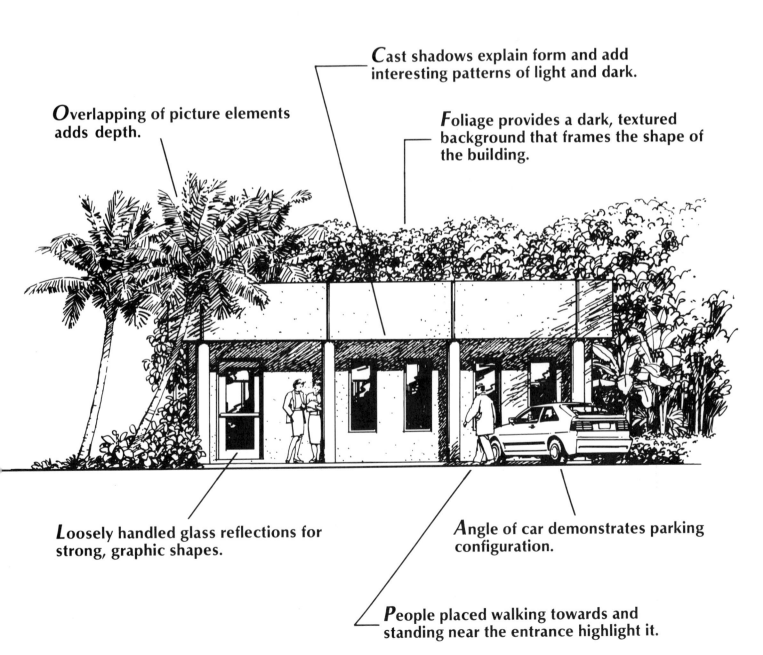

Cast shadows explain form and add interesting patterns of light and dark.

Overlapping of picture elements adds depth.

Foliage provides a dark, textured background that frames the shape of the building.

Loosely handled glass reflections for strong, graphic shapes.

Angle of car demonstrates parking configuration.

People placed walking towards and standing near the entrance highlight it.

*H*uman form has long
challenged the artist's creative
powers. Its irresistible force of
communication places it among
the foremost instruments of
graphic expression.

Stephen Rogers Peck
Atlas of Human Anatomy for the Artist

1/2"

1/2"

3/8"

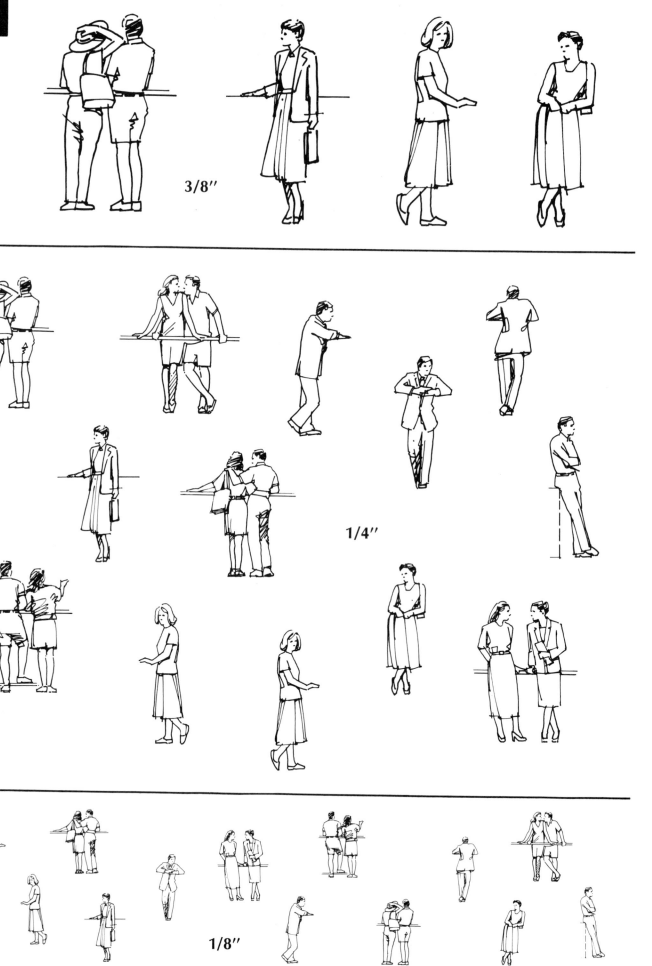

3/8″

1/4″

1/8″

1/2"

3/8"

1/4"

1/8"

also see pages 25-26, 45-47, 69-71

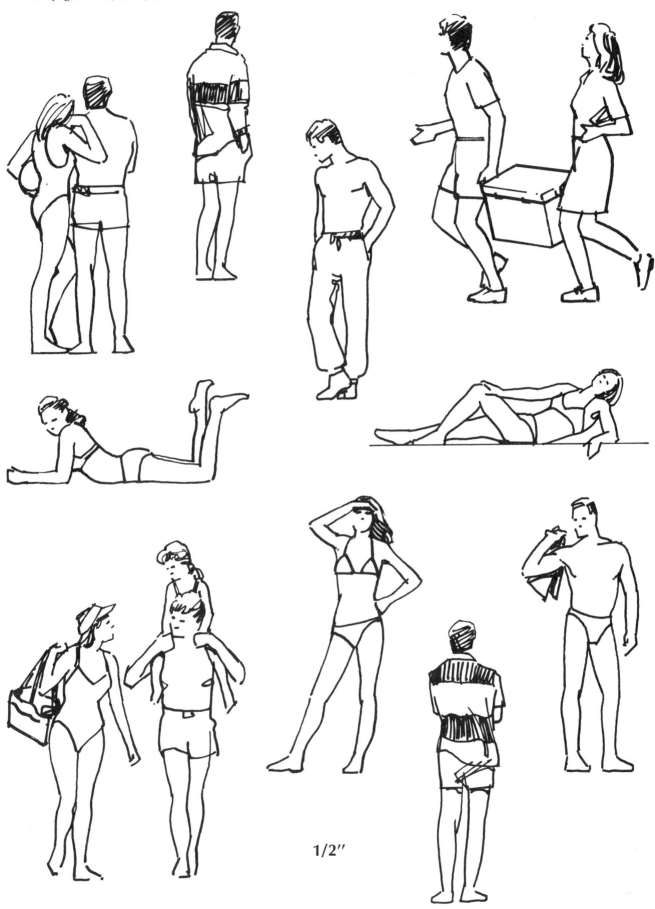

1/2"

3/8"

1/4"

1/8"

1/2"

24

3/8"

1/4"

1/8"

also see pages 35-36

1/2"

3/8"

1/4"

1/8"

1/2"

3/8''

1/4''

1/8''

1/2"

3/8"

1/4"

1/8"

1/2"

3/8"

1/4"

1/8"

also see pages 56-57, 65

1/2''

3/8''

1/4''

1/8''

1/2″

1/2″

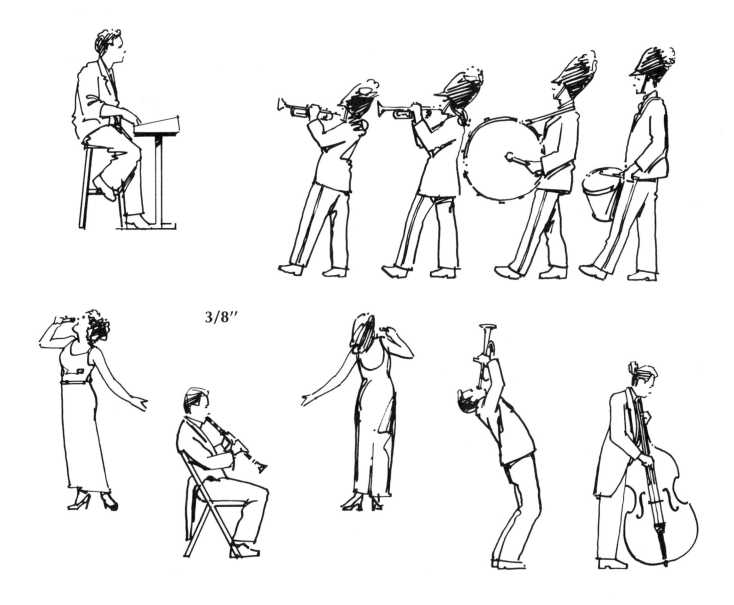

3/8″

3/8″

1/4″

1/8″

also see pages 21-26

1/2"

3/8"

1/4"

1/8"

Handicapped People

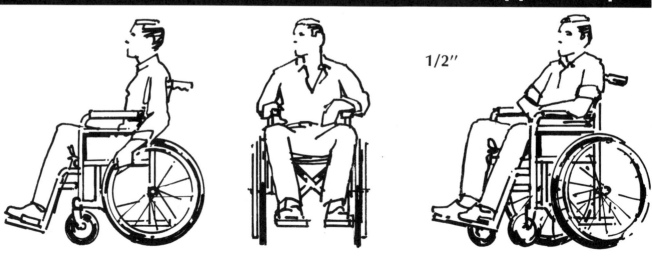

1/2"

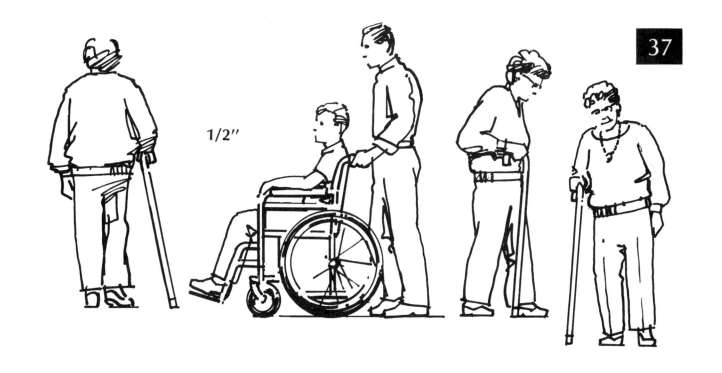

1/2"

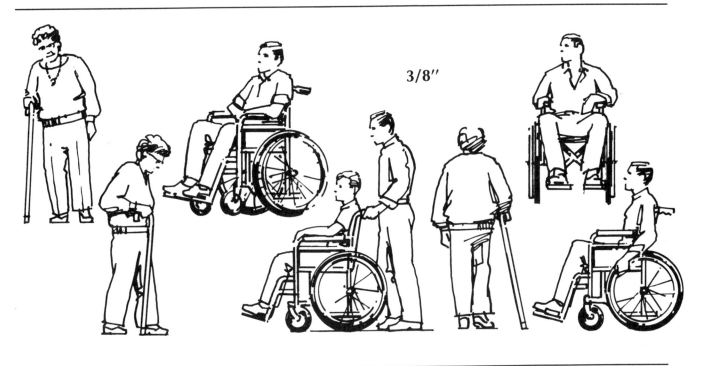

3/8"

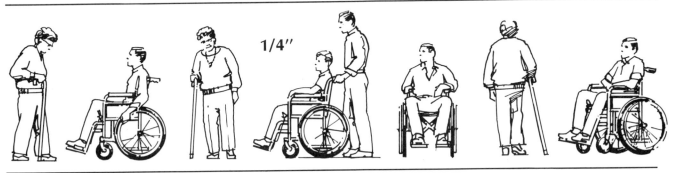

1/4"

1/8"

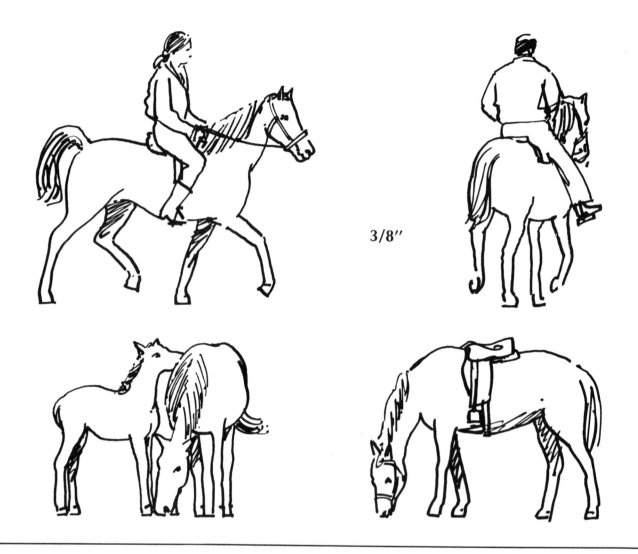

3/8"

1/4"

  1/8"

also see pages 54-55

1/2"

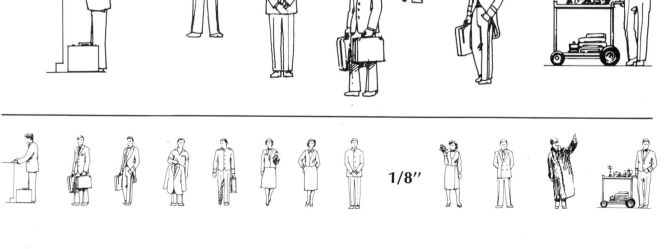

40

3/8"

1/4"

1/8"

also see pages 21-22

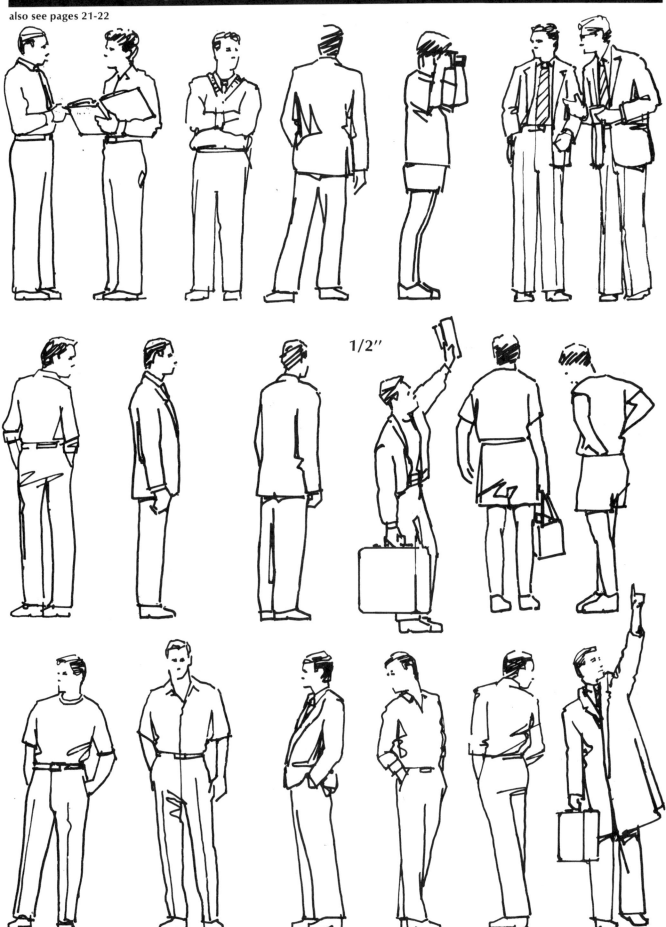

1/2"

1/2"

3/8"

3/8″

1/4″

1/8″

1/2"

1/2″

3/8″

3/8"

1/4"

1/4″

1/8″

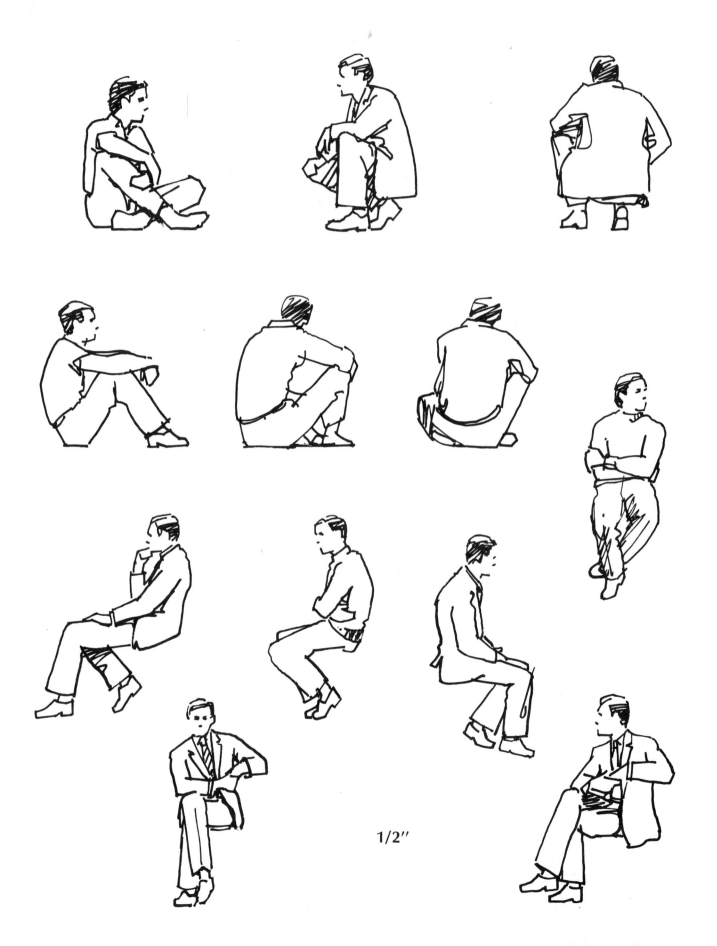

1/2"

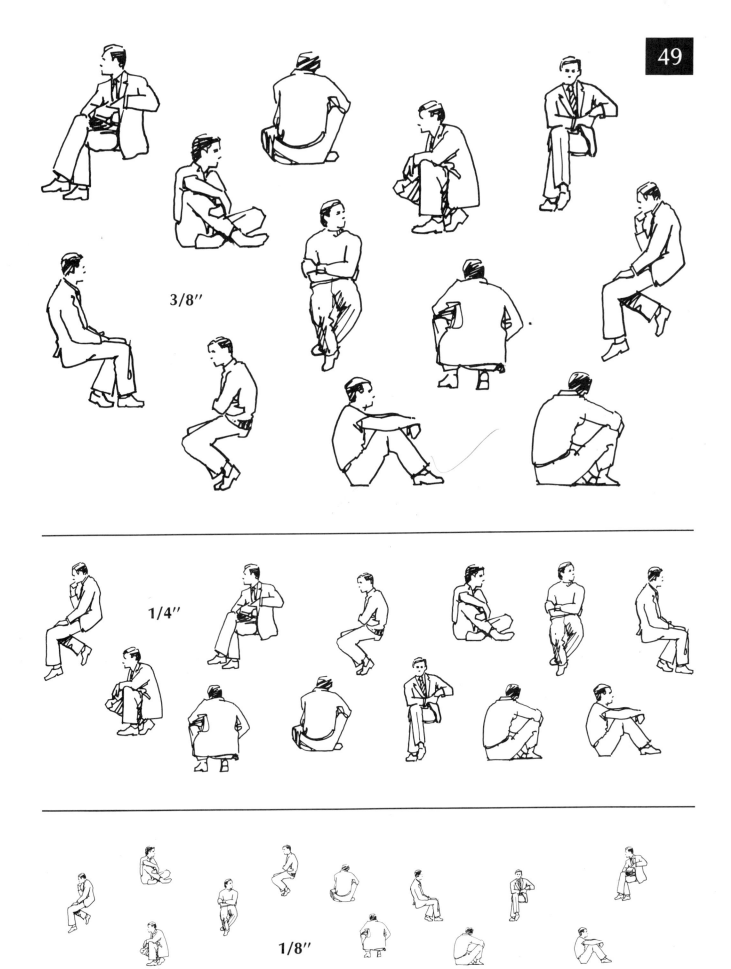

3/8"

1/4"

1/8"

1/2″

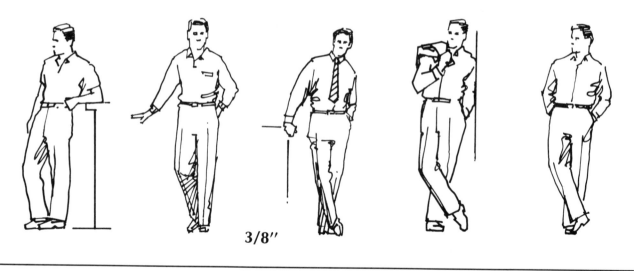

3/8″

1/4″

1/8″

also see pages 54-55

1/2"

3/8″

1/4″

1/8″

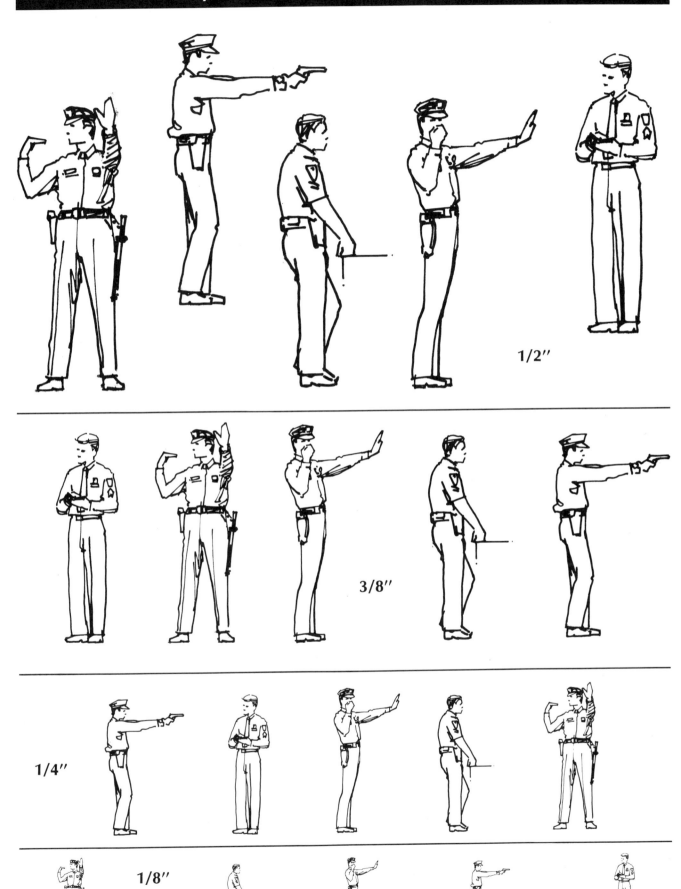

1/2"

3/8"

1/4"

1/8"

1/2″

3/8"

1/4"

1/8"

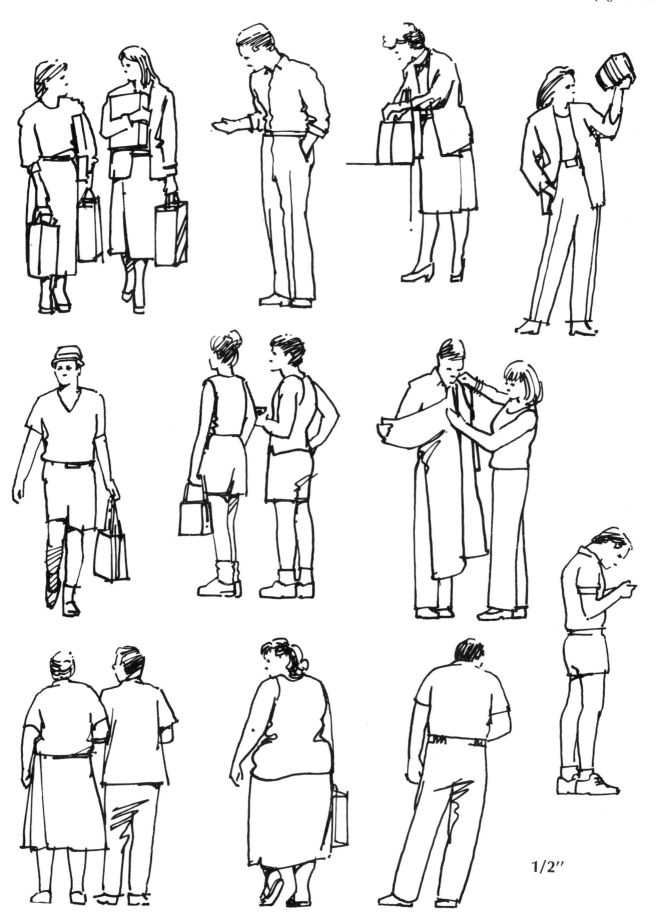

1/2"

3/8"

1/4"

1/8"

3/8"

1/2"

1/4"

1/8"

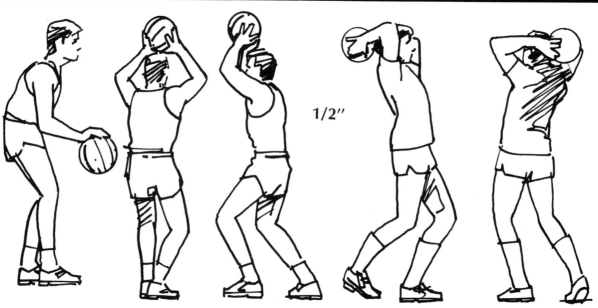

1/2"

3/8″

1/4″

1/8″

Sports-Fishing

1/8″

1/2″

3/8″

1/4″

1/8"

1/4"

3/8"

1/2"

also see page 105

1/2″

3/8″

1/4″

1/8″

1/2″

3/8″

1/4″

1/8″

Sports-Running

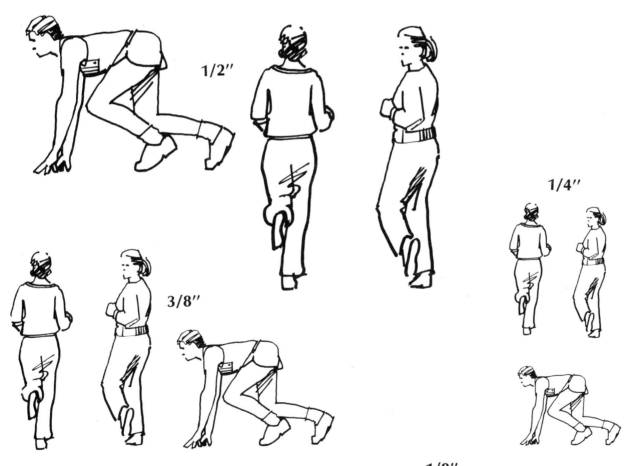

1/2″

1/4″

3/8″

1/8″

THE SURREY INSTITUTE OF ART & DESIGN

Farnham Campus, Falkner Road, Farnham, Surrey GU9 7DS

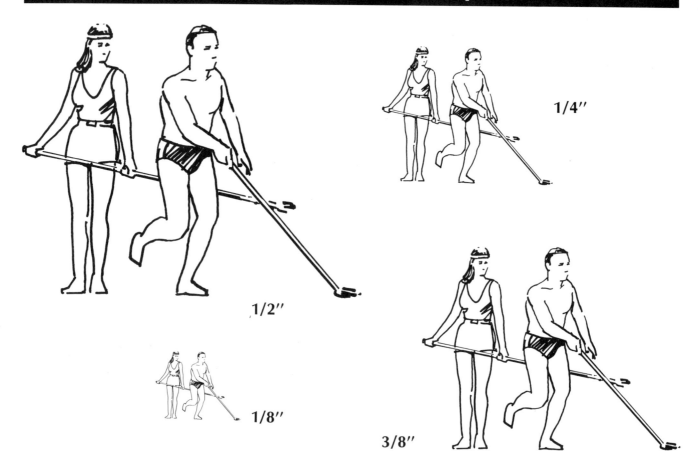

1/4″

1/2″

1/8″

3/8″

Sports-Skiing

1/8″

1/4″

3/8″

1/2″

1/2"

3/8"

1/4"

1/8"

1/2"

3/8"

1/4"

1/8"

1/2"

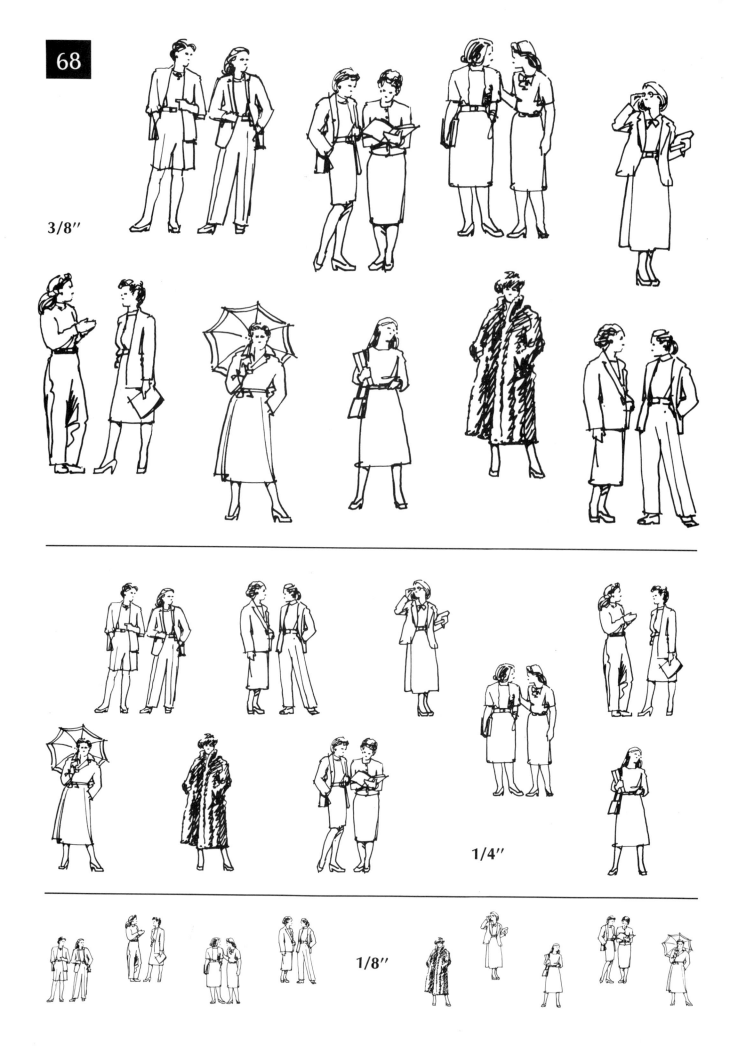

68

3/8″

1/4″

1/8″

1/2"

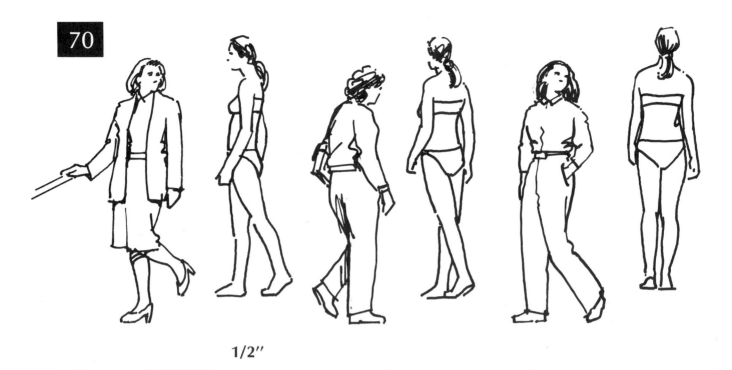

1/2''

3/8''

3/8″

1/4″

1/8″

1/2''

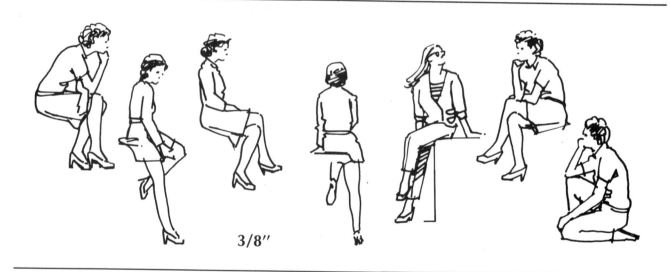

3/8''

1/4''

    1/8''

also see pages 16-18

1/2"

3/8"

1/4"

1/8"

It is in the nature of the
automobile that the city spreads
out thus and far away.

Frank Lloyd Wright
America Tomorrow

Vehicles

Rolls Royce

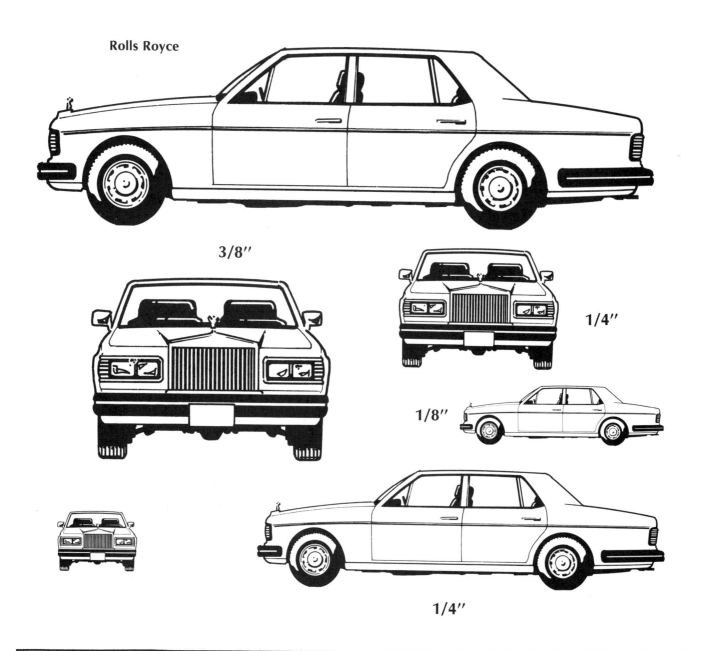

3/8″

1/4″

1/8″

1/4″

Volvo Coupe

3/8″

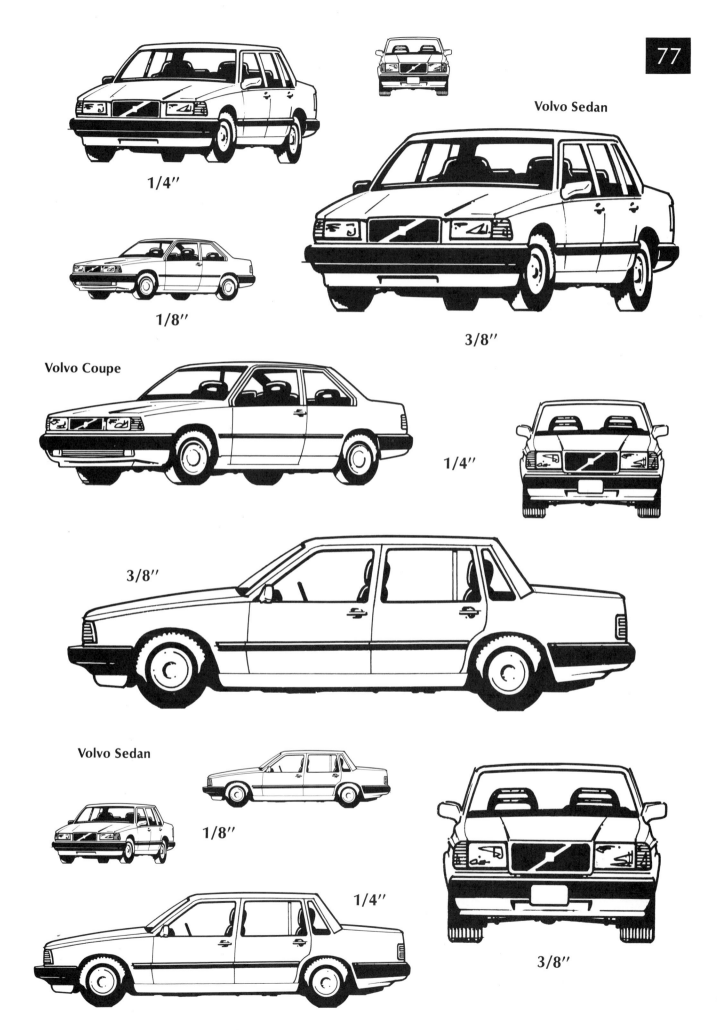

Volvo Sedan

1/4''

1/8''

3/8''

Volvo Coupe

1/4''

3/8''

Volvo Sedan

1/8''

1/4''

3/8''

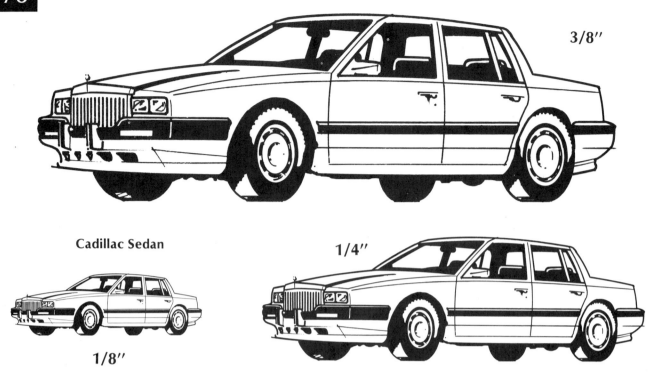

3/8"

Cadillac Sedan

1/4"

1/8"

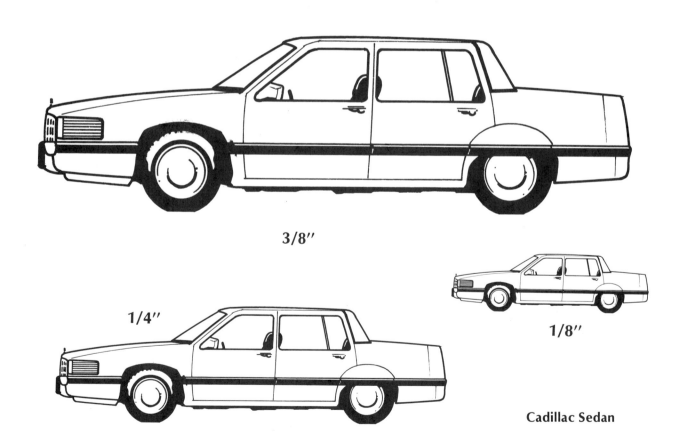

3/8"

1/4"

1/8"

Cadillac Sedan

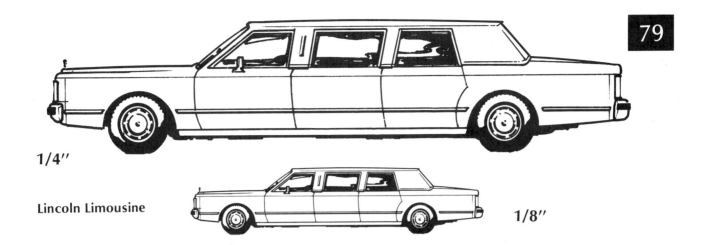

1/4"

Lincoln Limousine

1/8"

Family Cars

Chevrolet Sedan

3/8"

Chevrolet Coupe

Chevrolet Sedan   **1/4″**

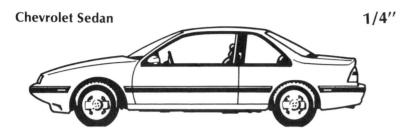

Chevrolet Coupe

1/8″

3/8″

Chevrolet Sedan

1/4″

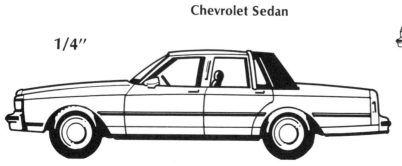

1/8″

Chevrolet Station Wagon

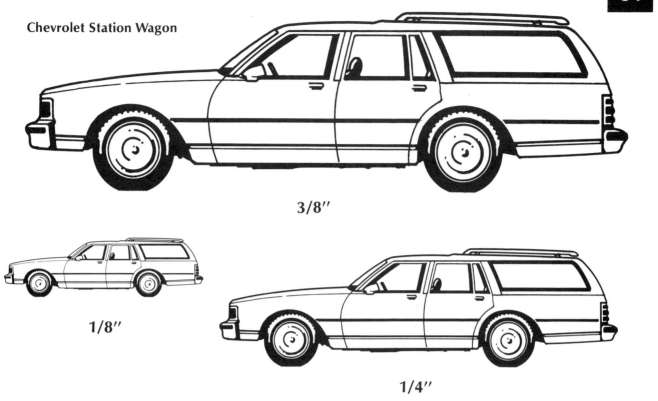

3/8″

1/8″

1/4″

3/8″

Volkswagen Station Wagon

1/4″

1/8″

3/8"

Volkswagen Station Wagon

1/4"

1/8"

3/8"

1/8"

1/4"

Volkswagen Coupe

3/8"

1/8″

1/4″

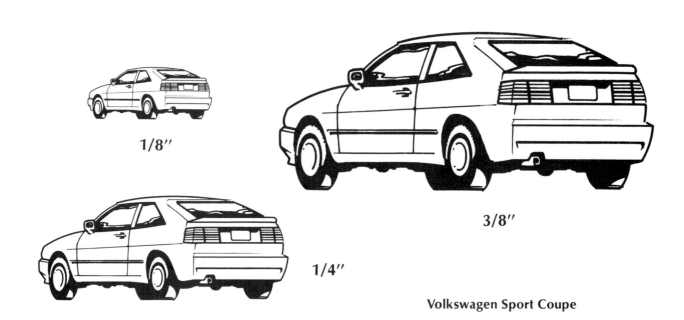

1/8″

3/8″

1/4″

Volkswagen Sport Coupe

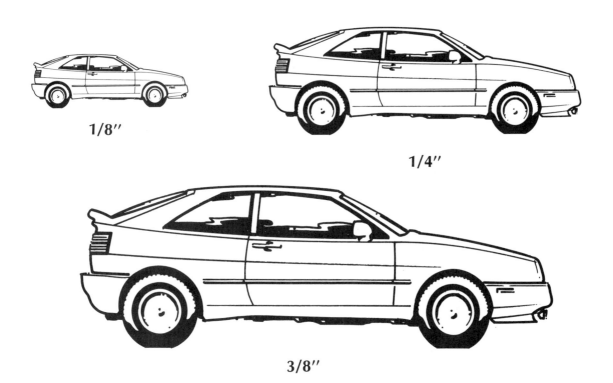

1/8″

1/4″

3/8″

Porsche

1/4''

3/8''

1/4''

1/8''

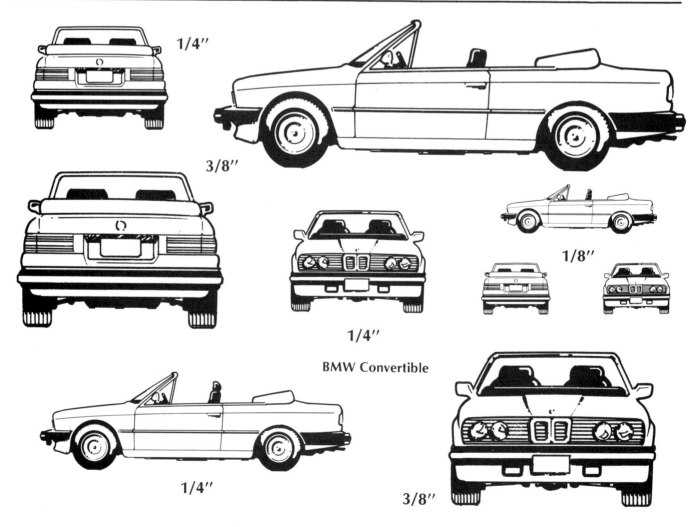

1/4''

3/8''

1/8''

1/4''

BMW Convertible

1/4''

3/8''

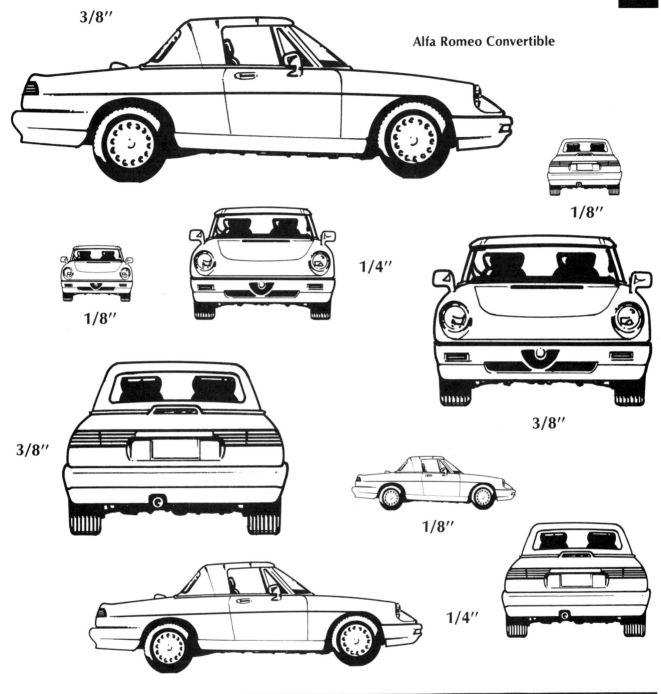

3/8''

Alfa Romeo Convertible

1/8''

1/4''

1/8''

3/8''

3/8''

1/8''

1/4''

3/8''

Porsche Convertible

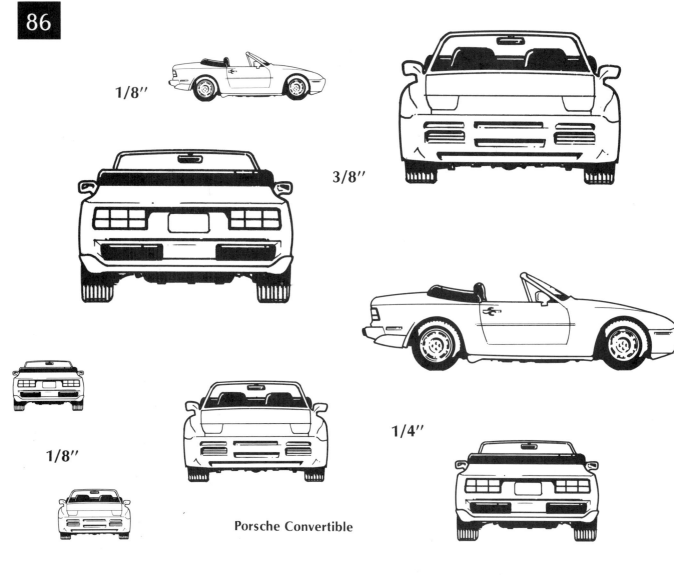

1/8″

3/8″

1/4″

1/8″

Porsche Convertible

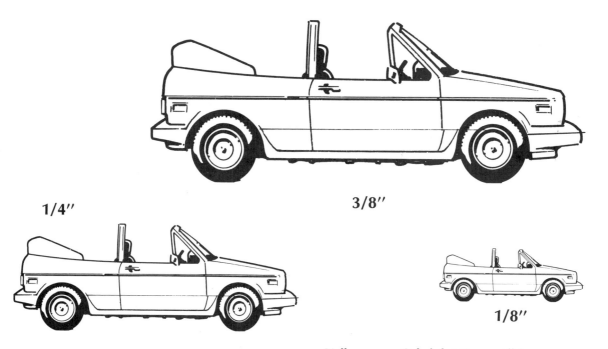

1/4″

3/8″

1/8″

Volkswagen Cabriolet Convertible

3/8″　　　**Chevrolet Camaro Z-28**

1/4″

1/8″

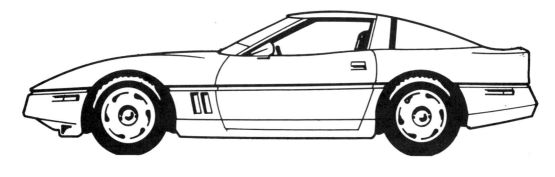

Chevrolet Corvette

3/8″

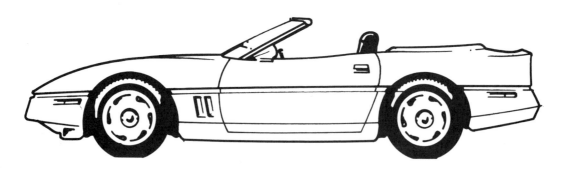

1/4″

1/8″

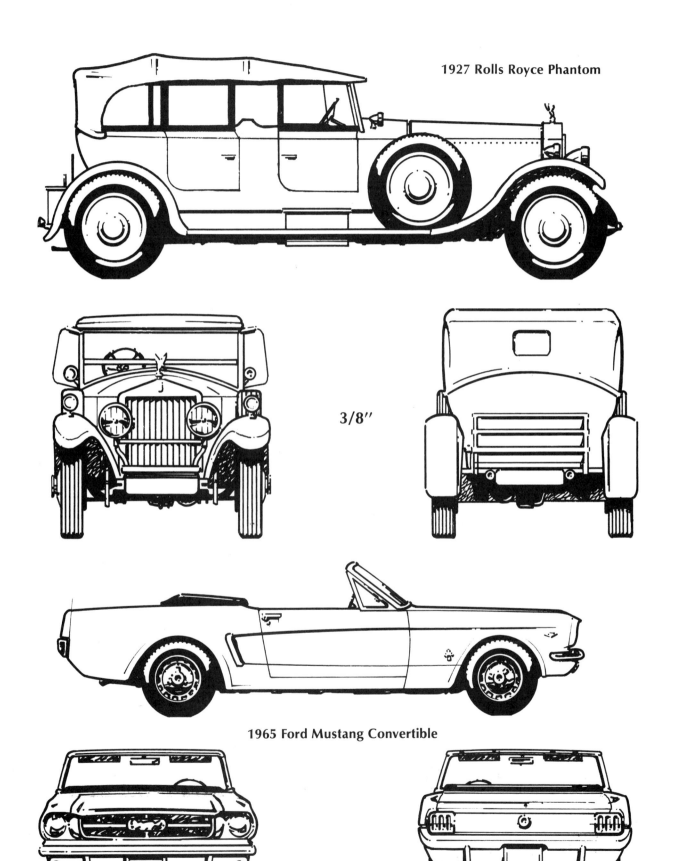

1927 Rolls Royce Phantom

3/8"

1965 Ford Mustang Convertible

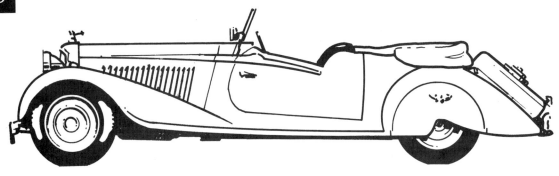

1939 Bentley

3/8"

1955 Citroën

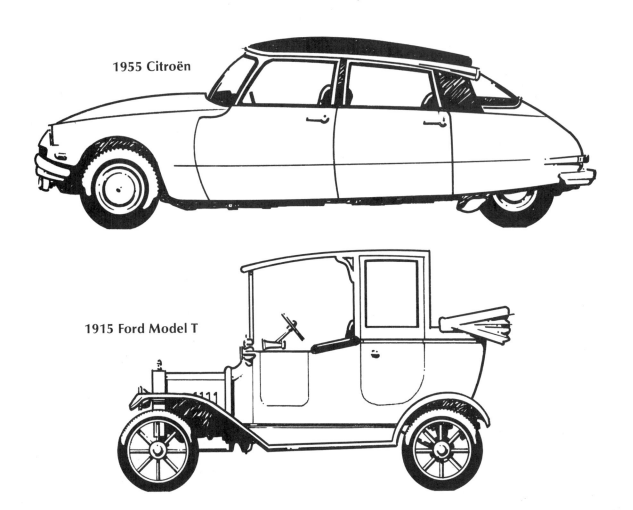

1915 Ford Model T

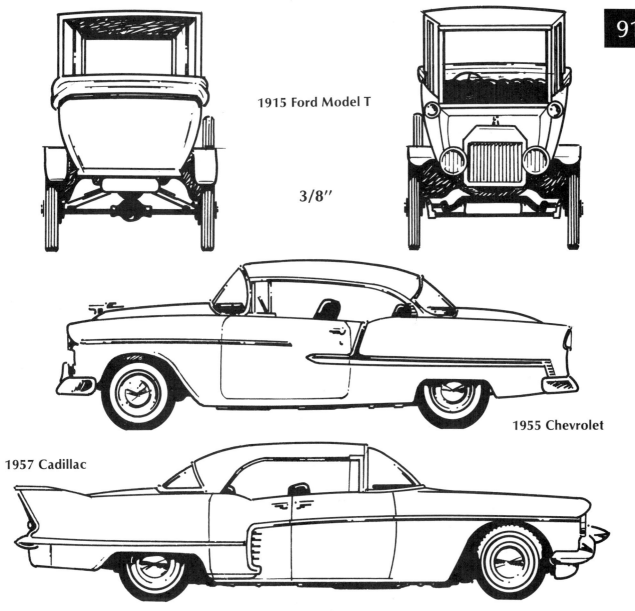

1915 Ford Model T

3/8″

1955 Chevrolet

1957 Cadillac

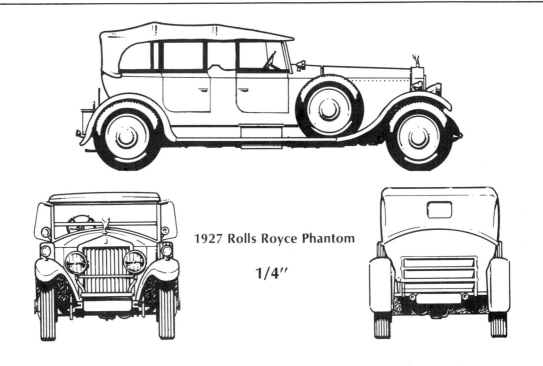

1927 Rolls Royce Phantom

1/4″

1957 Cadillac

1939 Bentley

1/4"

1955 Citroën

1915 Ford Model T

1955 Chevrolet

1/4″

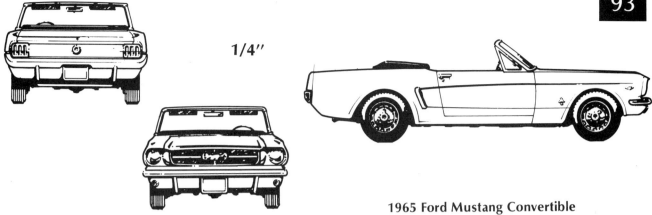

1965 Ford Mustang Convertible

1/8″

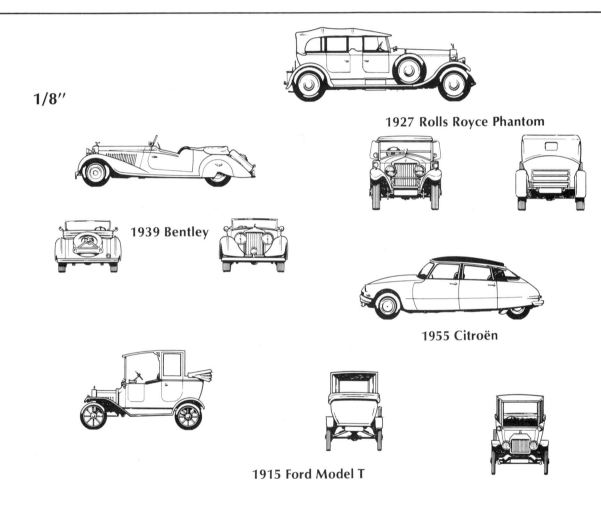

1927 Rolls Royce Phantom

1939 Bentley

1955 Citroën

1915 Ford Model T

1955 Chevrolet

1957 Cadillac

1965 Ford Mustang Convertible

3/8''

Chevrolet Pickup

1/4''

Chevrolet Pickup

1/4"

1/8"

Chevrolet Lumina Passenger Van

3/8"

3/8″

Chevrolet Lumina Passenger Van

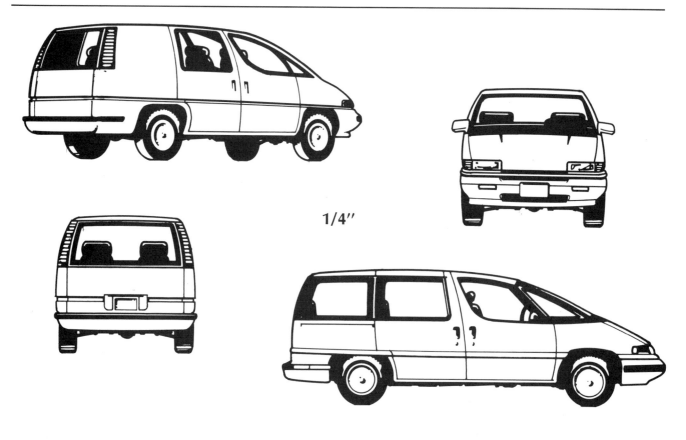

1/4″

1/8″

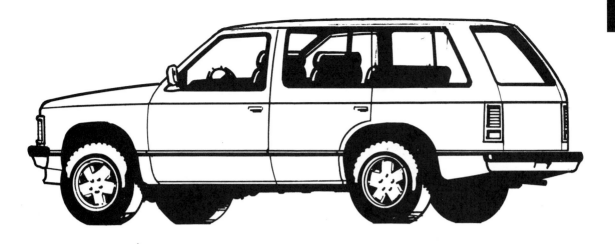

Chevrolet Blazer

3/8"

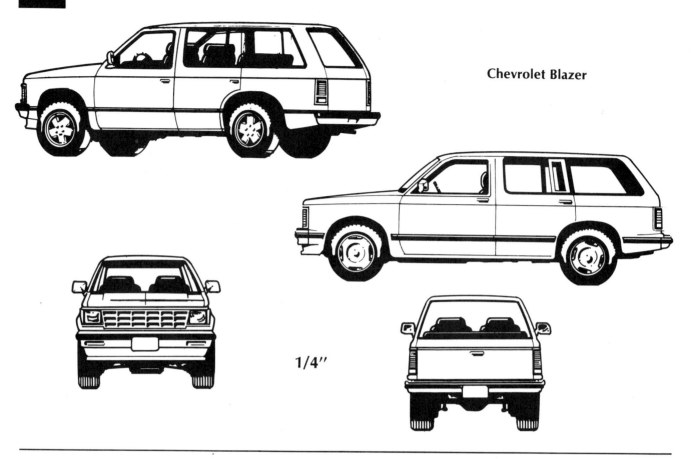

Chevrolet Blazer

1/4"

1/8"

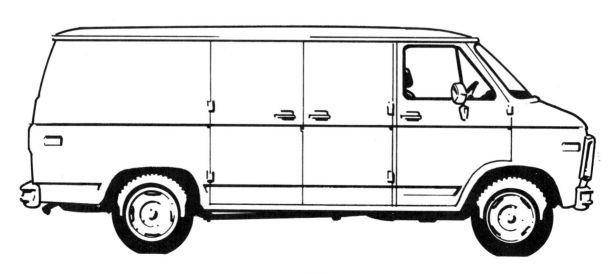

3/8"   **Chevrolet Cargo Van**

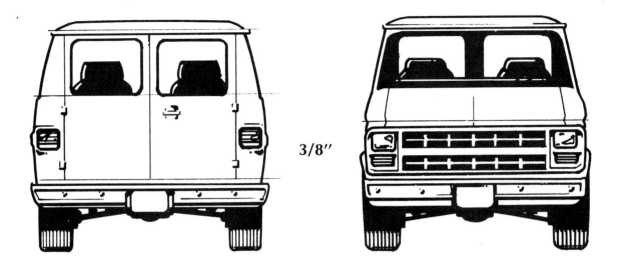

3/8″

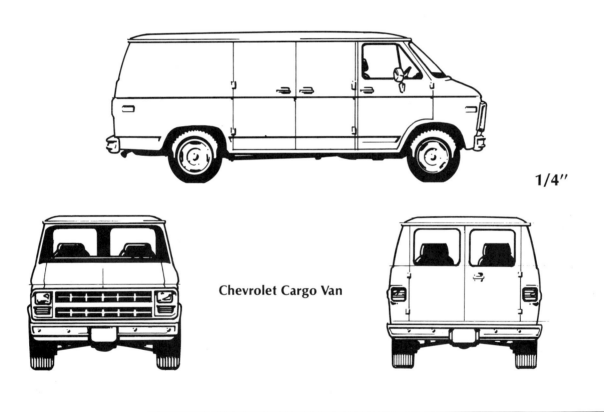

1/4″

Chevrolet Cargo Van

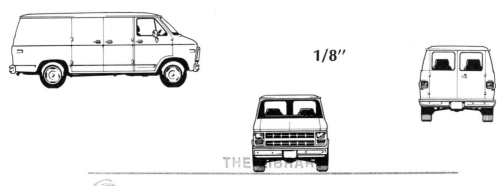

1/8″

Chevrolet Astro Passenger Van

3/8″

Chevrolet Astro Cargo Van

Chevrolet Astro Passenger Van

1/4″

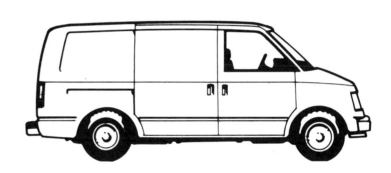

Chevrolet Astro Cargo Van

1/8″

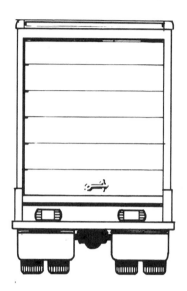

Isuzu Truck

1/4"

1/8"

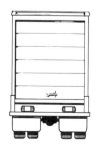

International Tractor

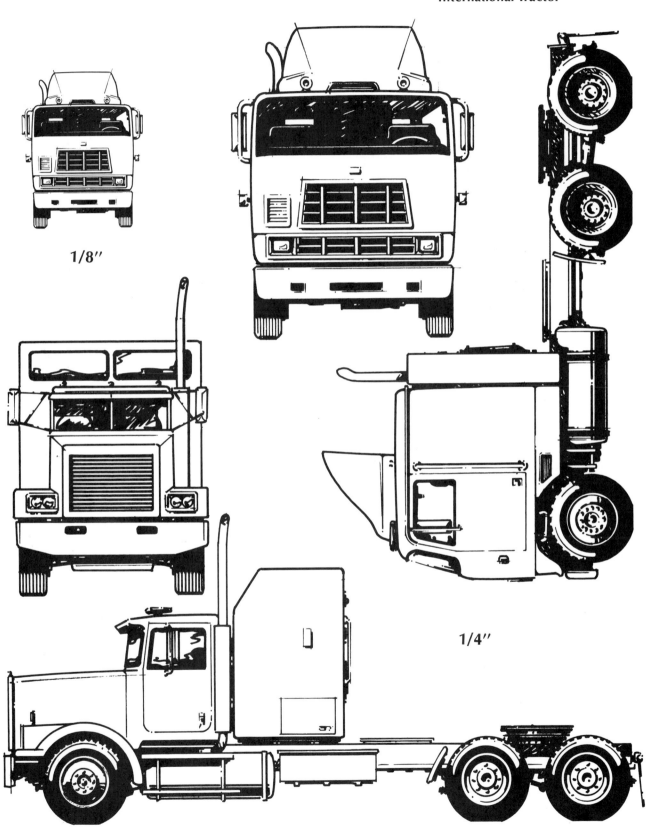

1/8″

1/4″

Kenworth Tractor

Tractors & Trailers

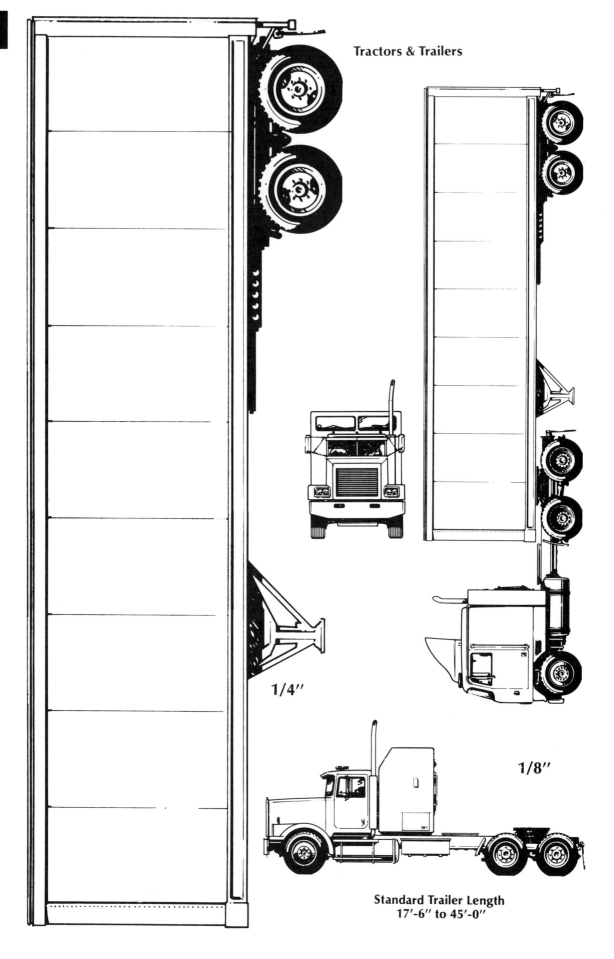

1/4"

1/8"

**Standard Trailer Length
17'-6" to 45'-0"**

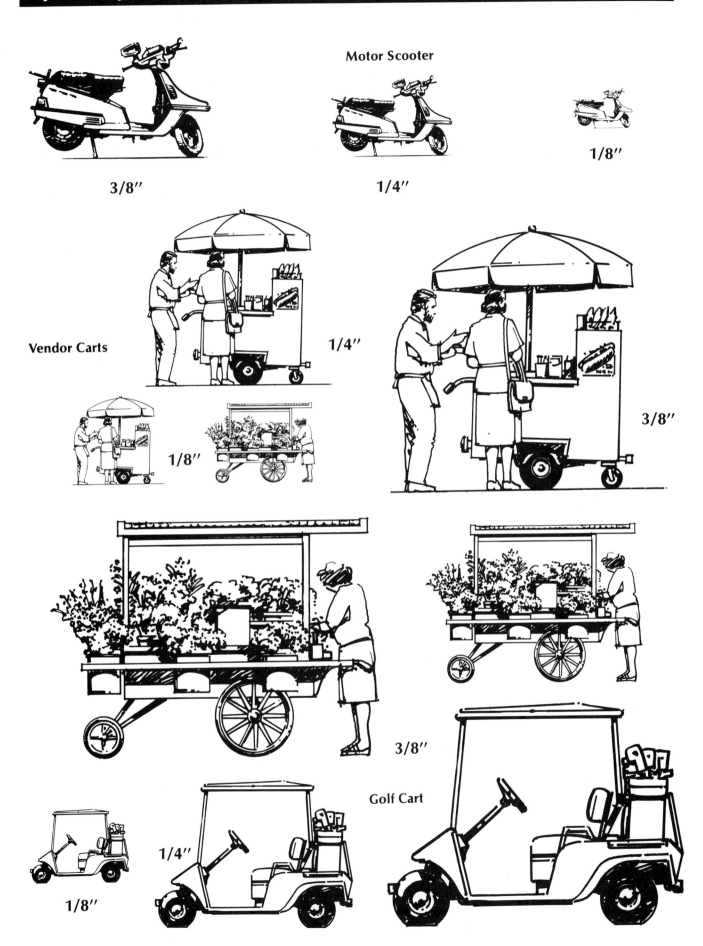

Motor Scooter

3/8"

1/4"

1/8"

Vendor Carts

1/4"

1/8"

3/8"

3/8"

Golf Cart

1/8"

1/4"

3/8"

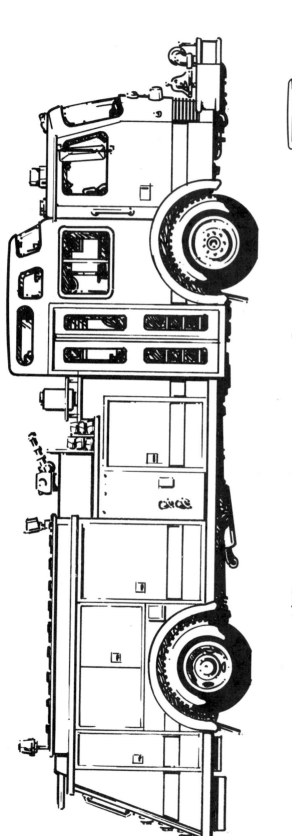

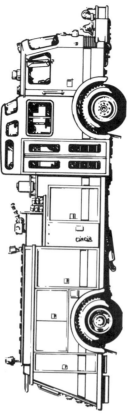

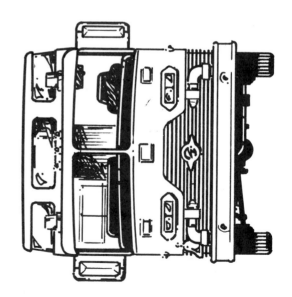

1/8''

Fire Engine

1/4''

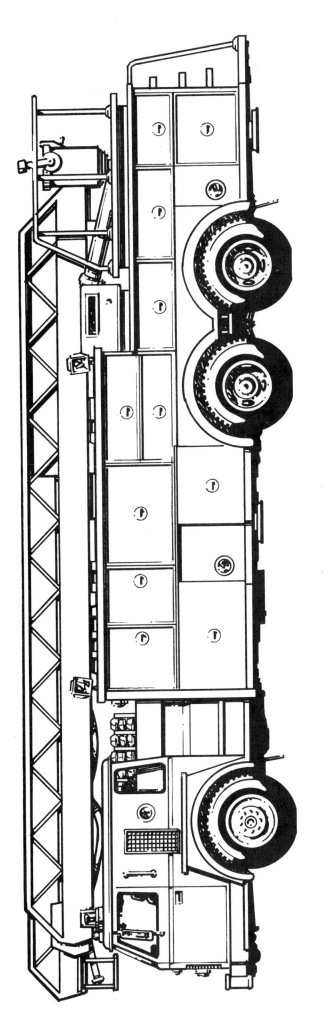

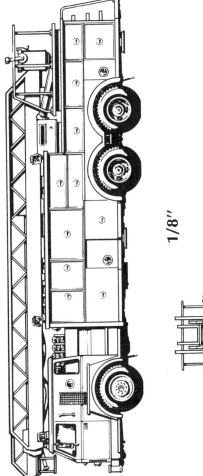

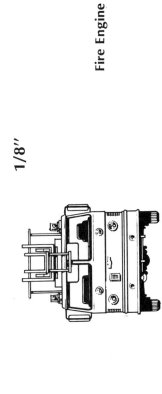

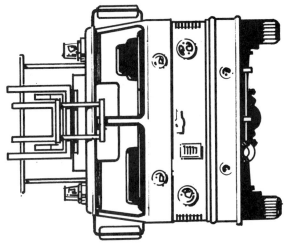

1/4"

1/8"

Fire Engine

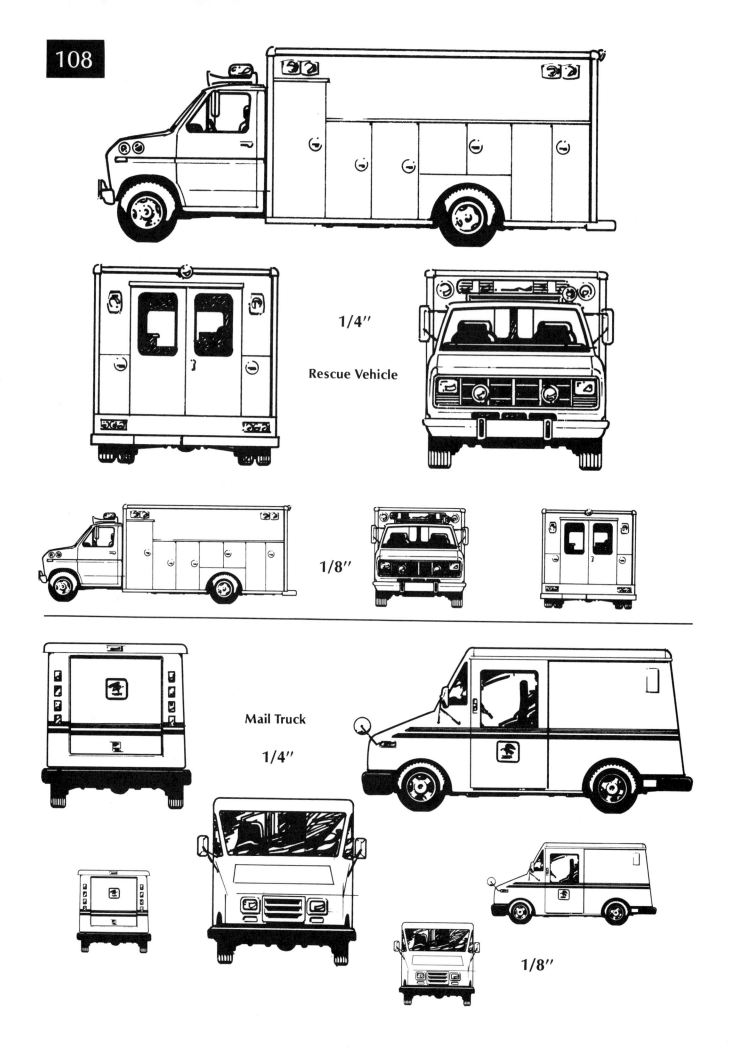

1/4″

Rescue Vehicle

1/8″

Mail Truck

1/4″

1/8″

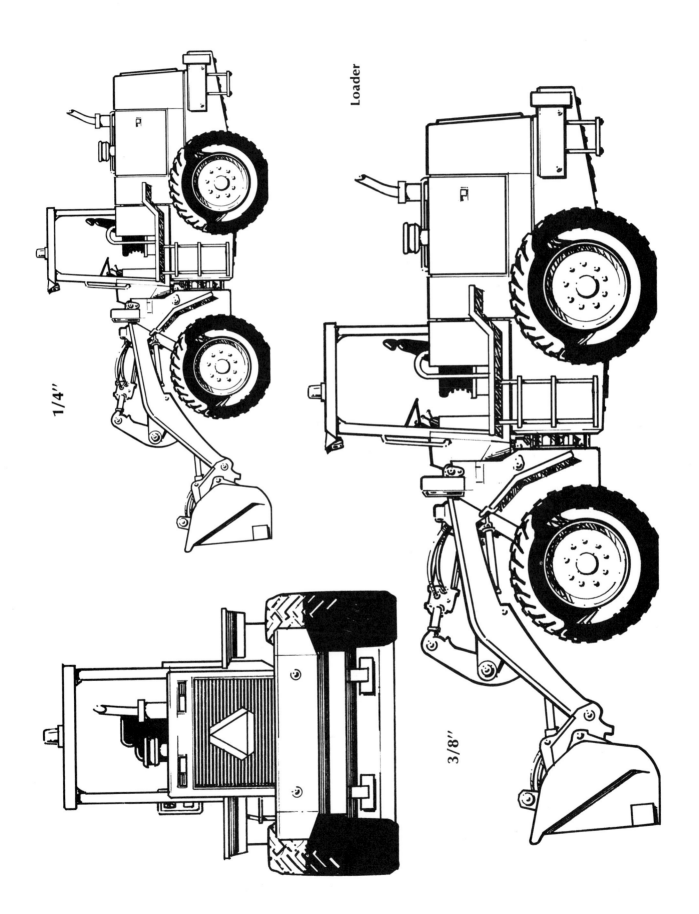

Loader

1/4"

3/8"

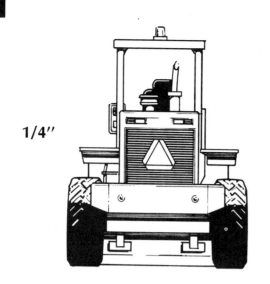

1/4"

Loader

1/8"

1/4"

Dump Truck

1/8"

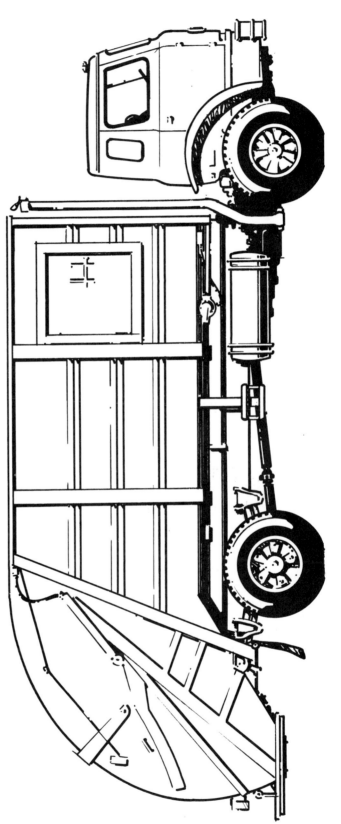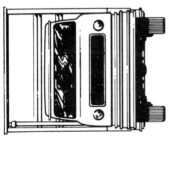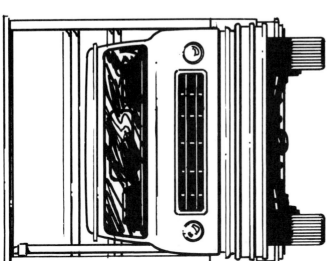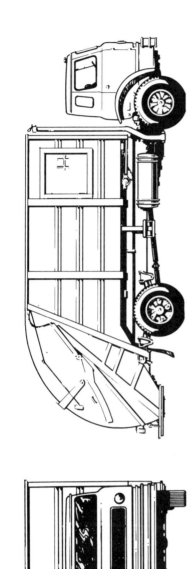

Garbage Truck

1/8''

1/4''

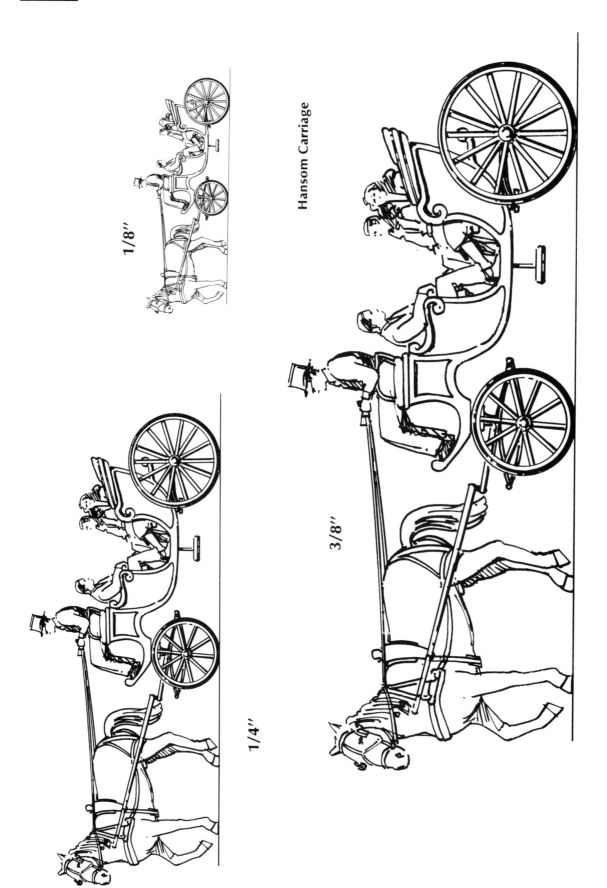

Hansom Carriage

1/8"

1/4"

3/8"

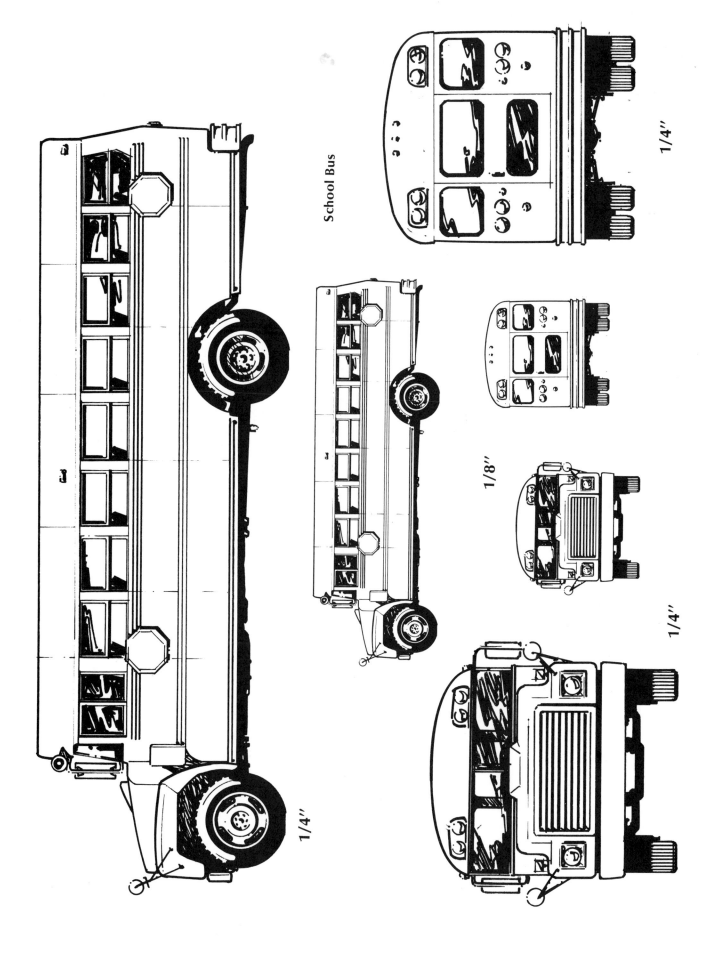

School Bus

1/4''

1/8''

1/4''

1/4''

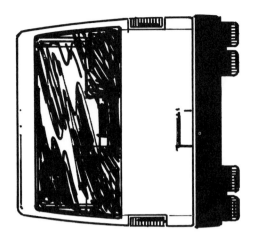

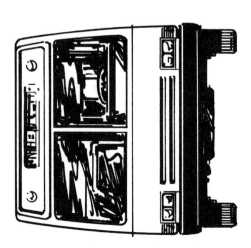

1/8"

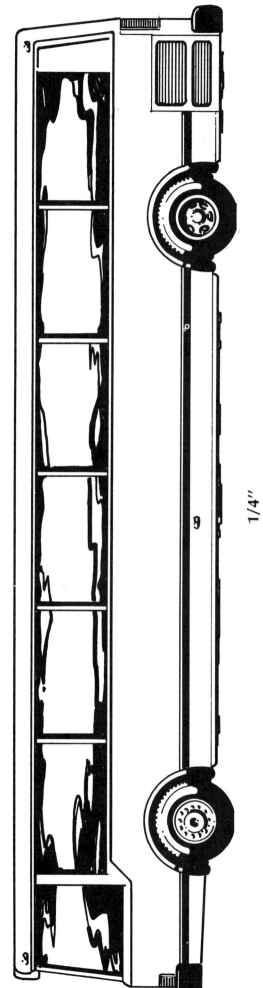

1/4"

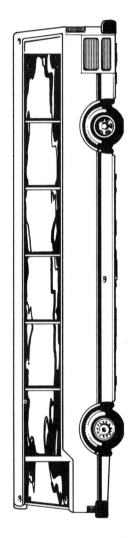

City Bus

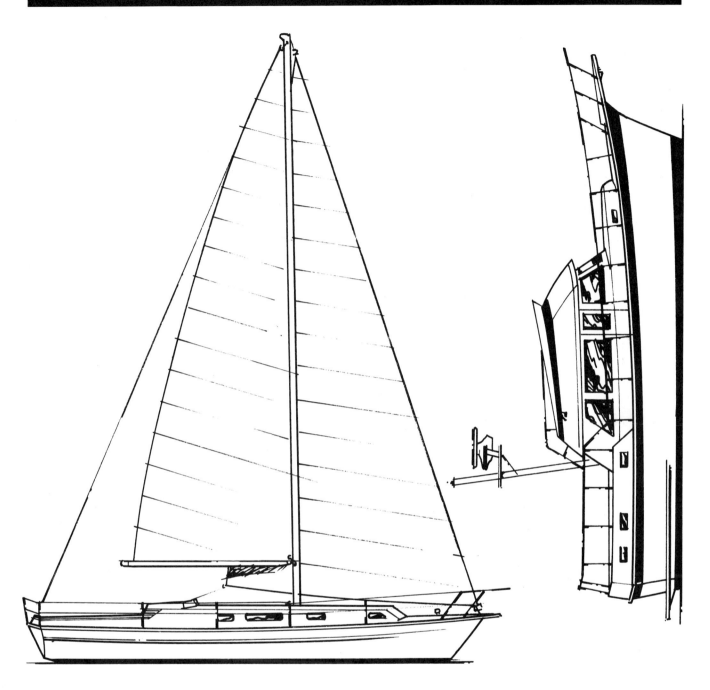

1/8"

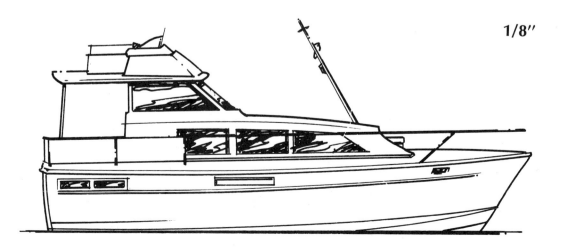

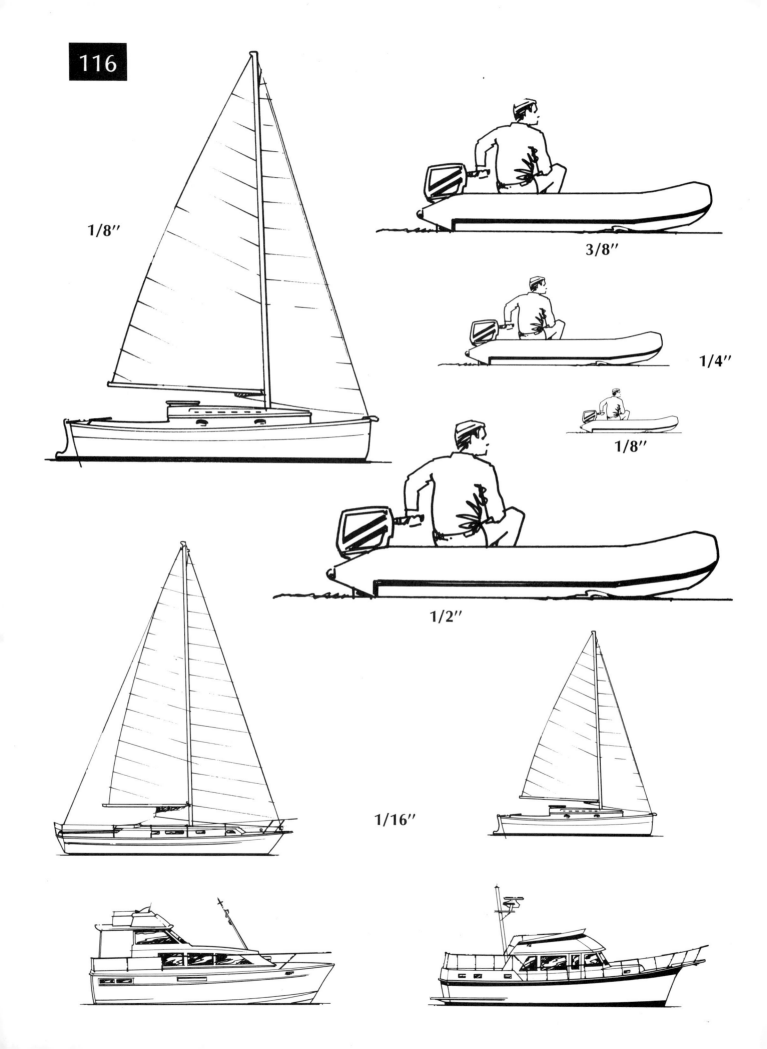

1/8″

3/8″

1/4″

1/8″

1/2″

1/16″

Boeing 727-200

1/16''

1''=30'

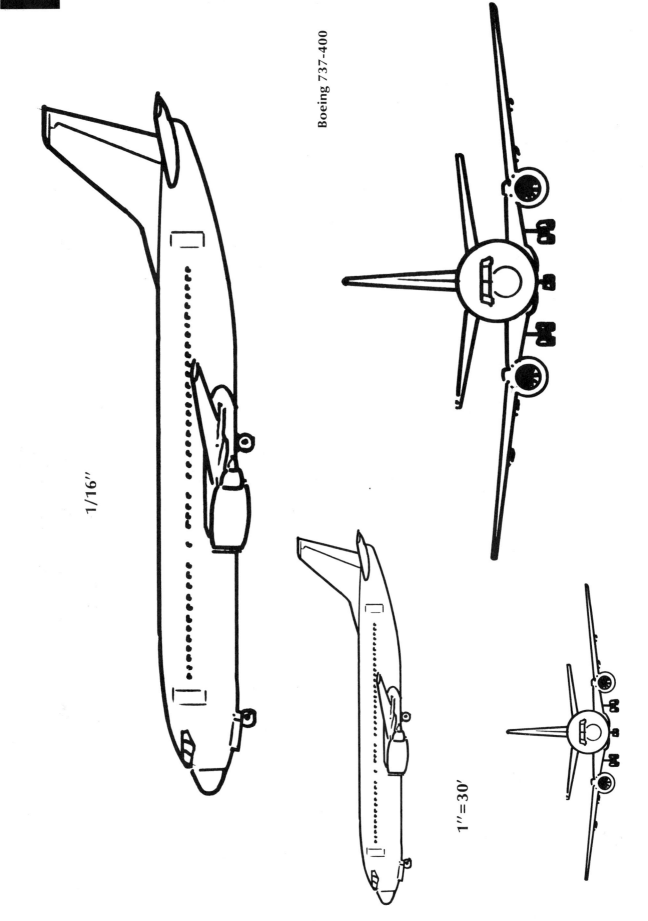

Boeing 737-400

1/16"

1"=30'

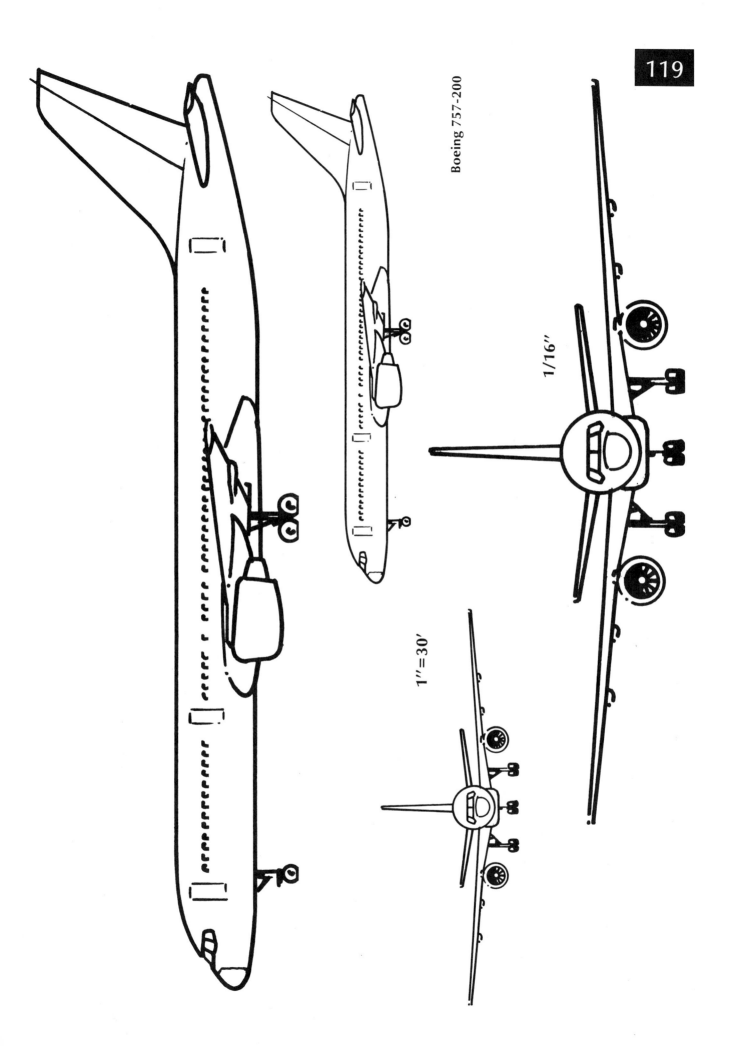

Boeing 757-200

1/16''

1''=30'

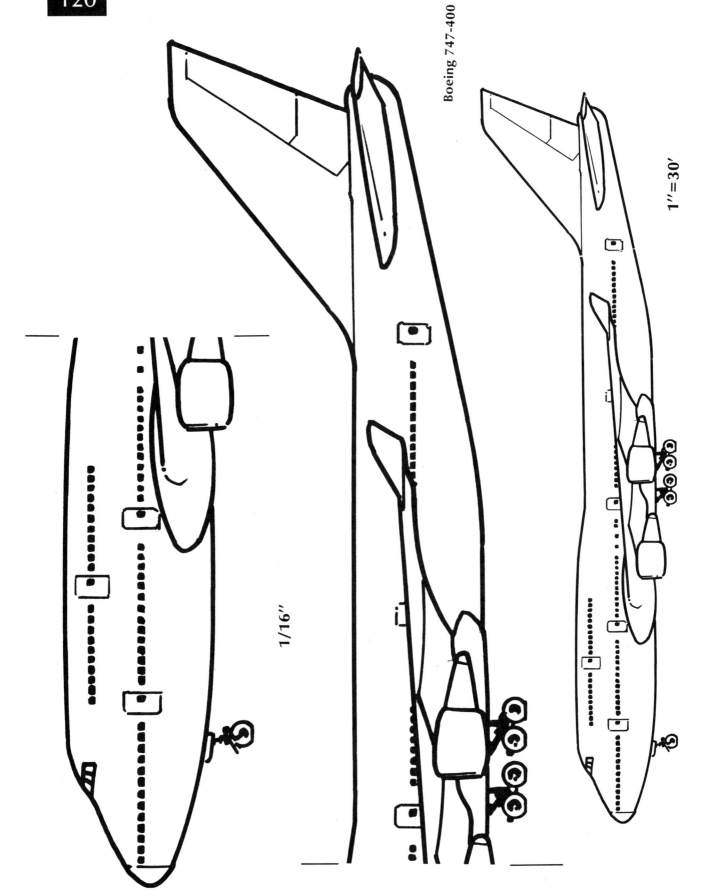

Boeing 747-400

1'' = 30'

1/16''

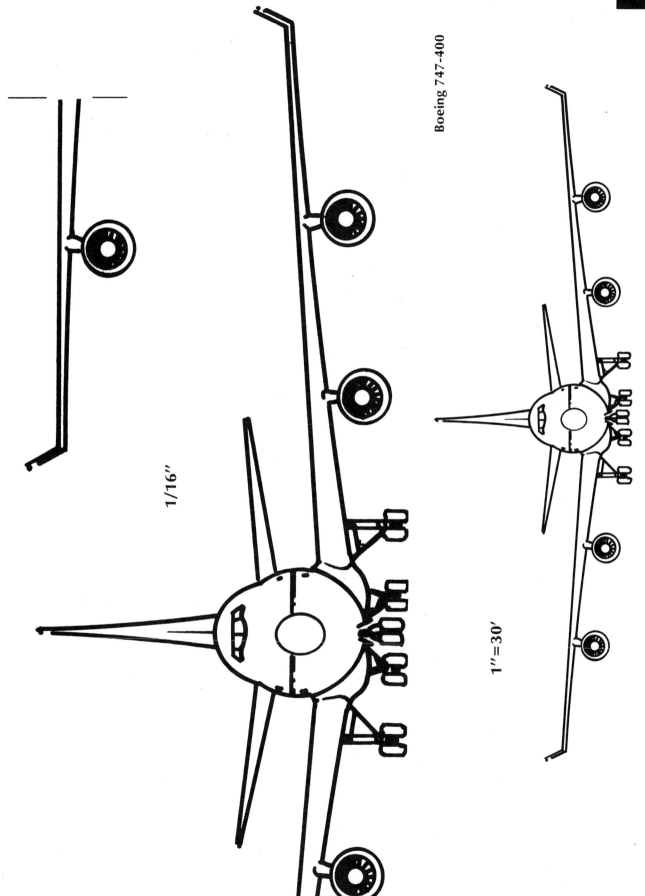

Boeing 747-400

1/16"

1"=30'

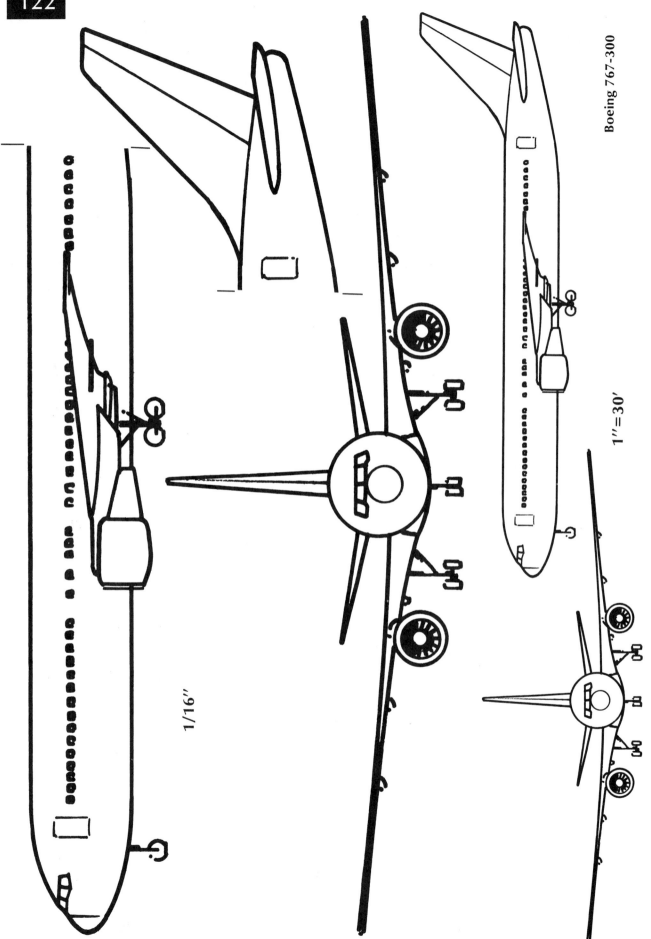

1/16''

1''=30'

Boeing 767-300

McDonnell Douglas DC-10, Series 300

1/16"

1" = 30'

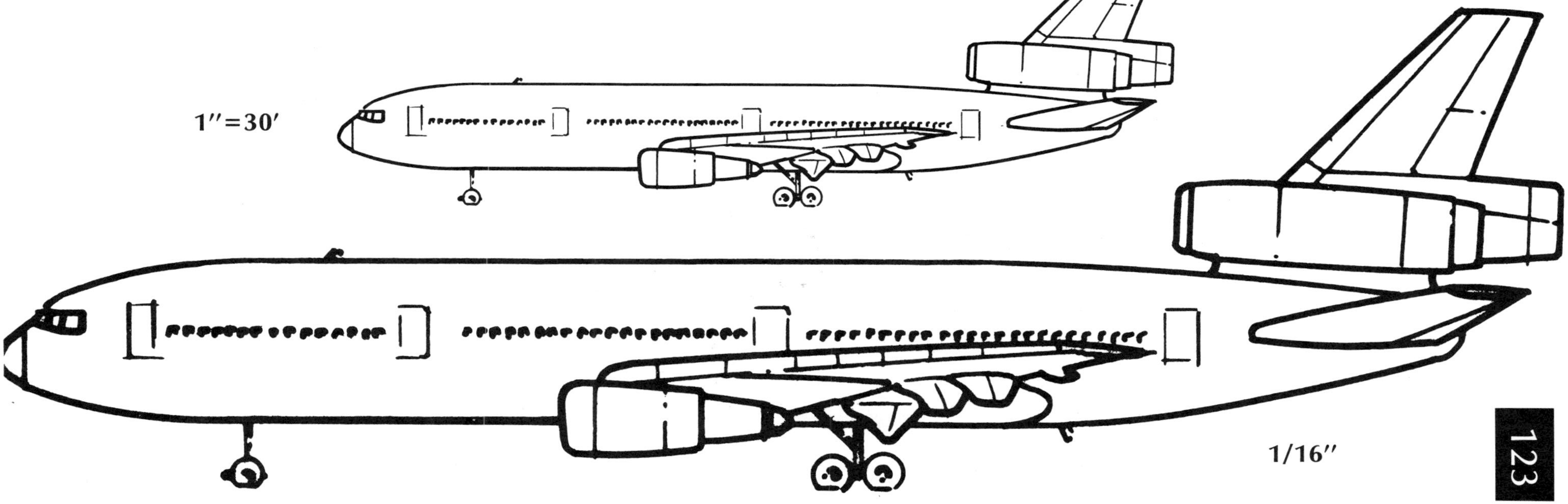

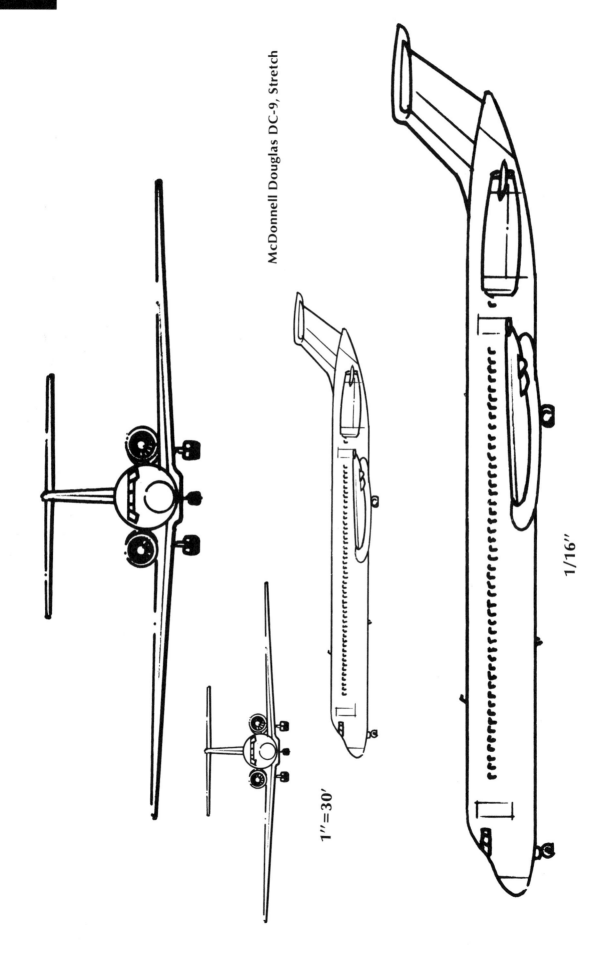

McDonnell Douglas DC-9, Stretch

1"=30'

1/16"

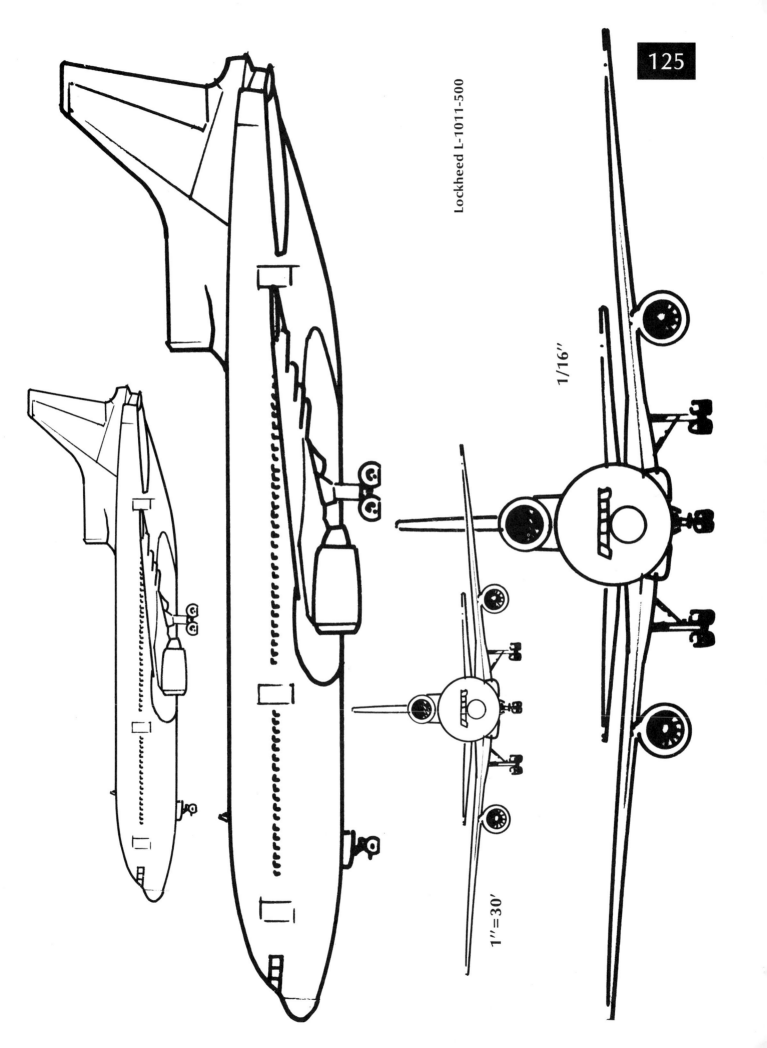

Lockheed L-1011-500

1/16"

1"=30'

125

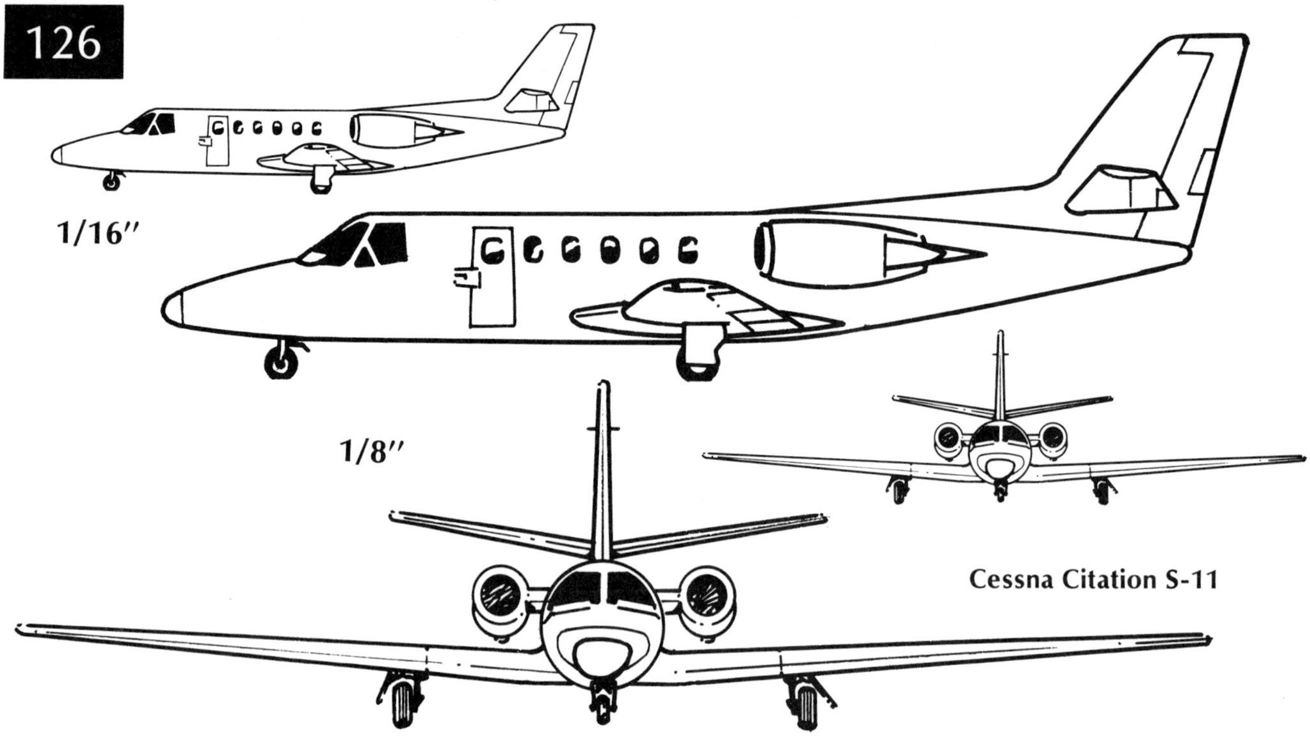

1/16″

1/8″

Cessna Citation S-11

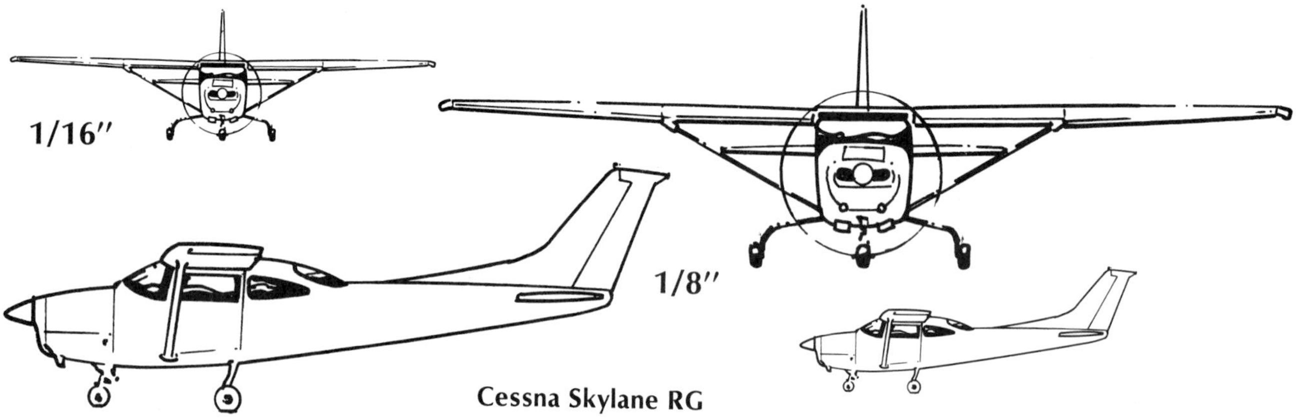

1/16″

1/8″

Cessna Skylane RG

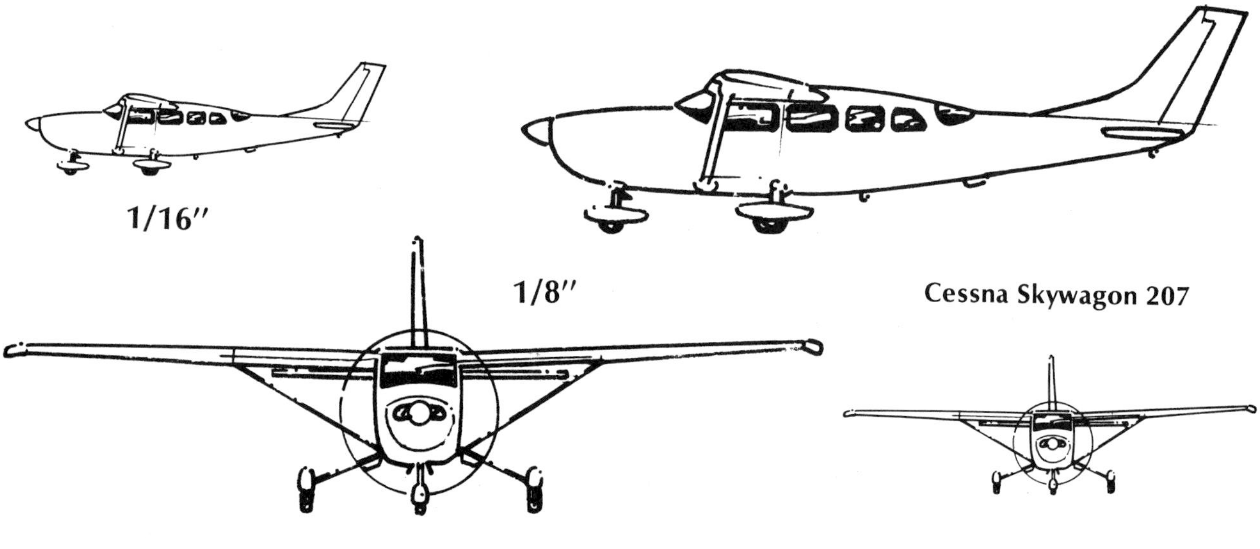

1/16″

1/8″

Cessna Skywagon 207

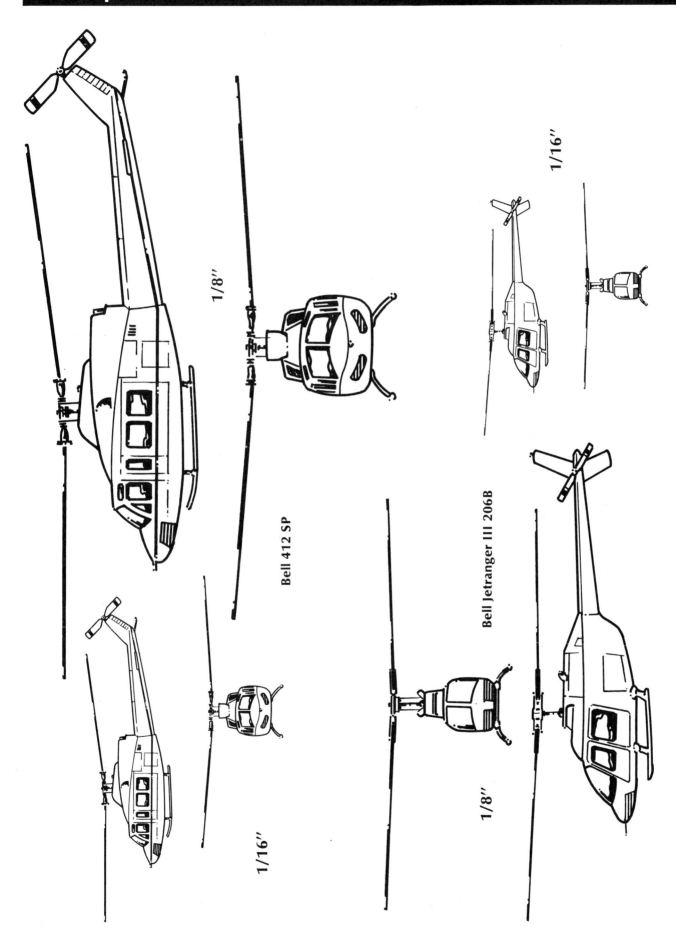

Bell 412 SP

1/8''

1/16''

Bell Jetranger III 206B

1/8''

1/16''

*H*uman observation and appreciation,
generally speaking, is gross; fine points are
unnoticed. Only impressive, dominant points of
any activity are remembered and recalled.
This permits the artist to paint only the essence
of an object or function in an illustration by
caricature...It is certain that a painting
of a South Seas palm tree, an umbrella,
a lounge chair, and a tall cool drink will
affect 90% of its viewers the same.
The other 10% doesn't drink.

Chris Choate
Architectural Presentation

Trees And Shrubs

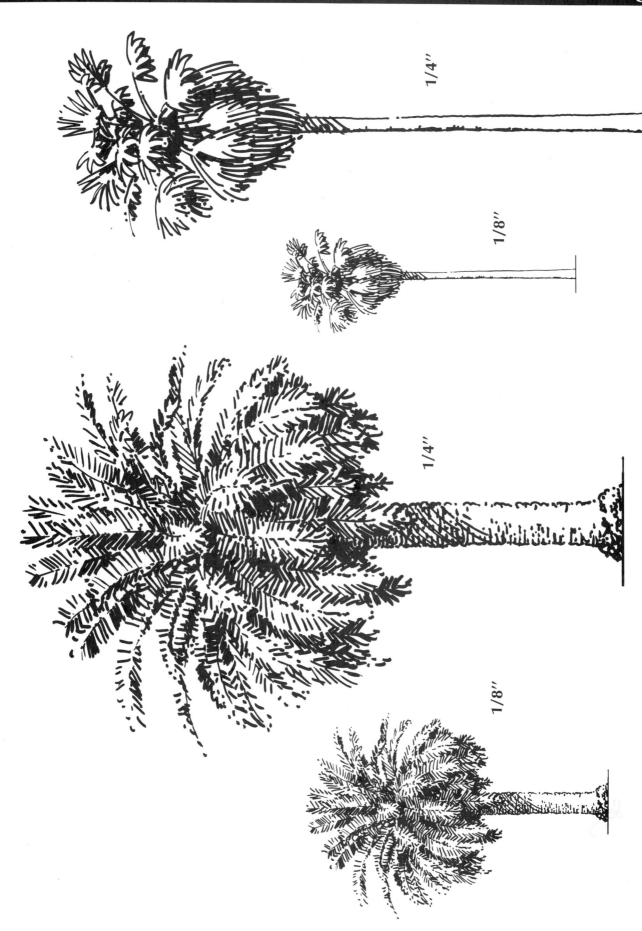

1/4"

1/8"

Fountain Palm (Livistona decipens)

1/4"

1/8"

Canary Island Date Palm (Phoenix canariensis)

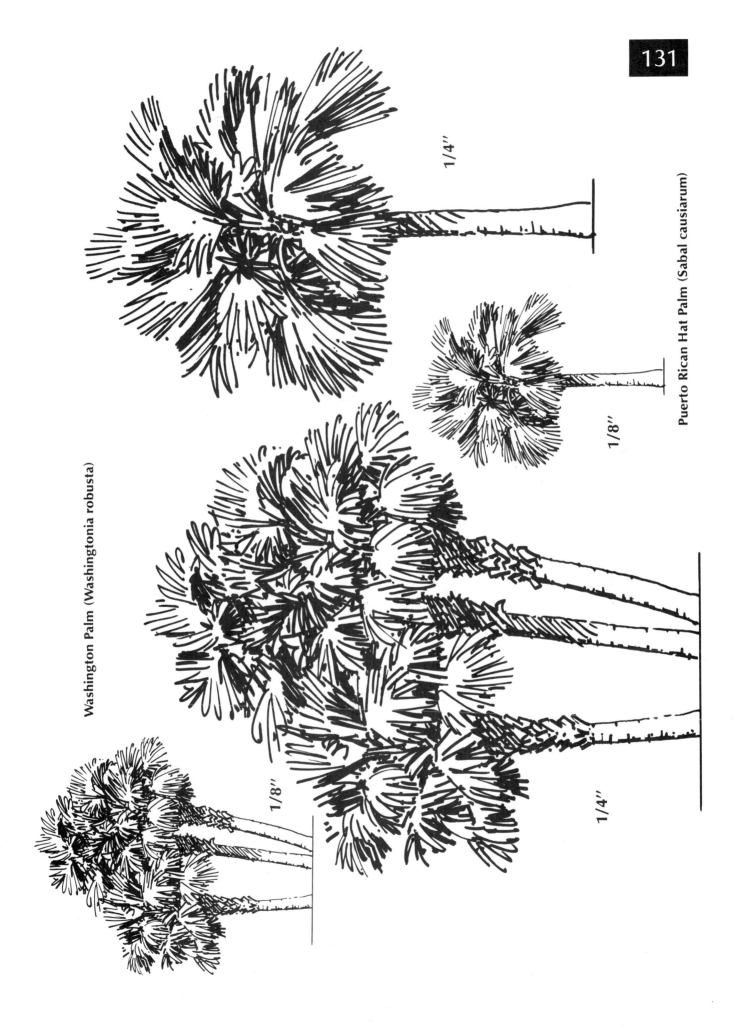

1/4"

Puerto Rican Hat Palm (Sabal causiarum)

1/8"

Washington Palm (Washingtonia robusta)

1/8"

1/4"

1/8"

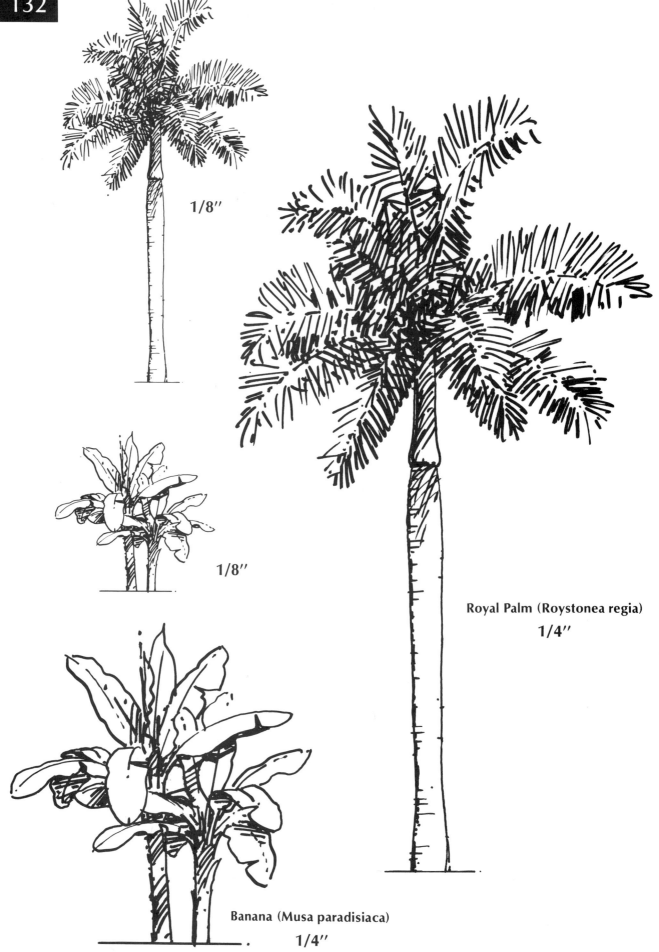

1/8″

1/8″

Royal Palm (Roystonea regia)
1/4″

Banana (Musa paradisiaca)
1/4″

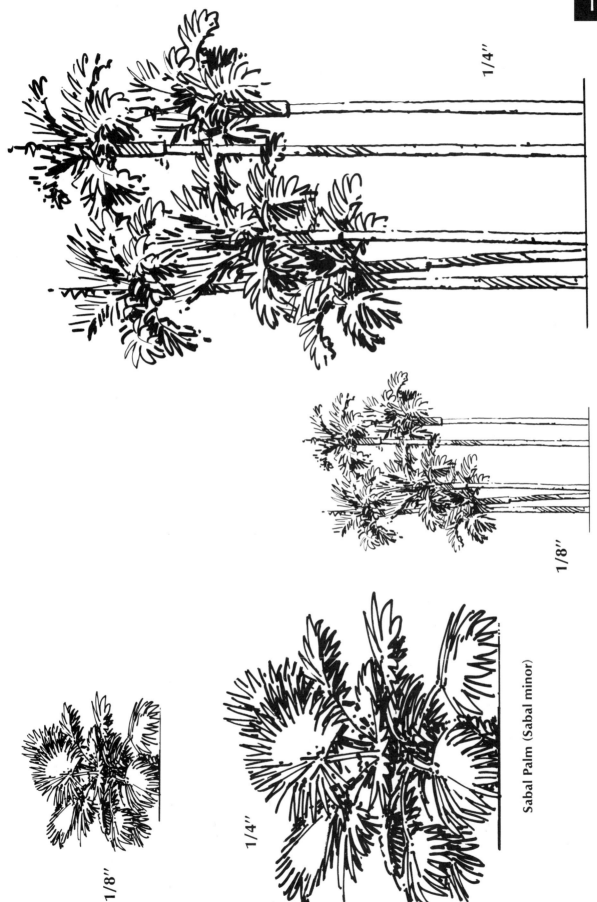

1/4"

Seaforthia Palm (Ptychosperma elegans)

1/8"

1/8"

1/4"

Sabal Palm (Sabal minor)

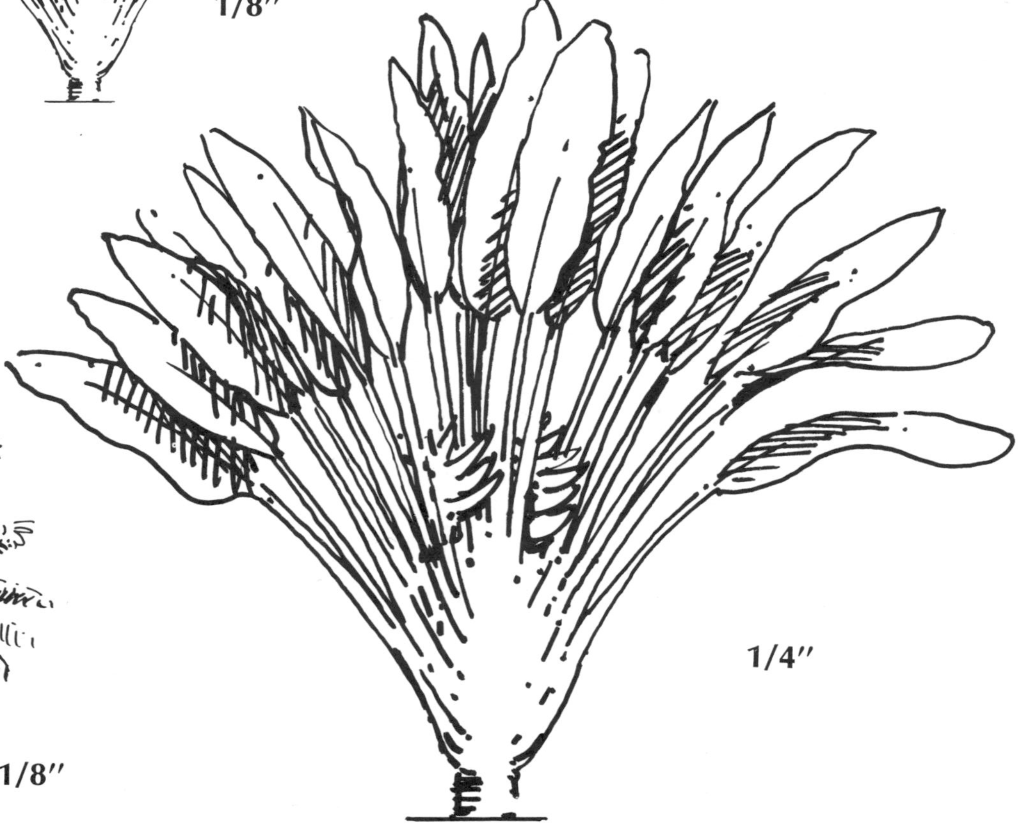

1/4"

Travelers Palm (Ravenala madagascariensis)

1/8"

1/8"

1/4"

Coconut Palm (Cocos nucifera)

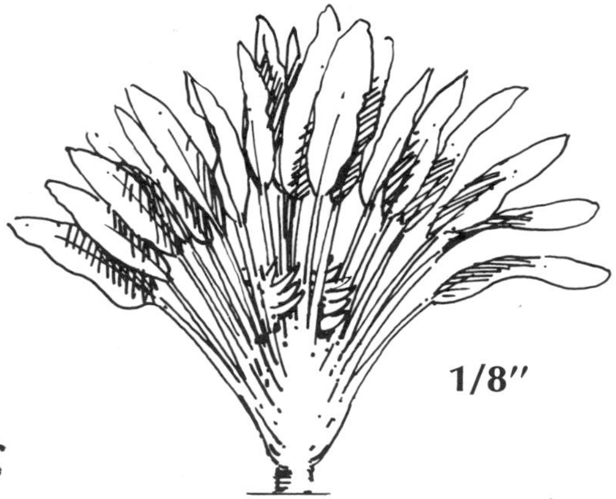

1/4"

Tropical Foliage
Background

1/8″

Tropical Foliage Background

3/16″

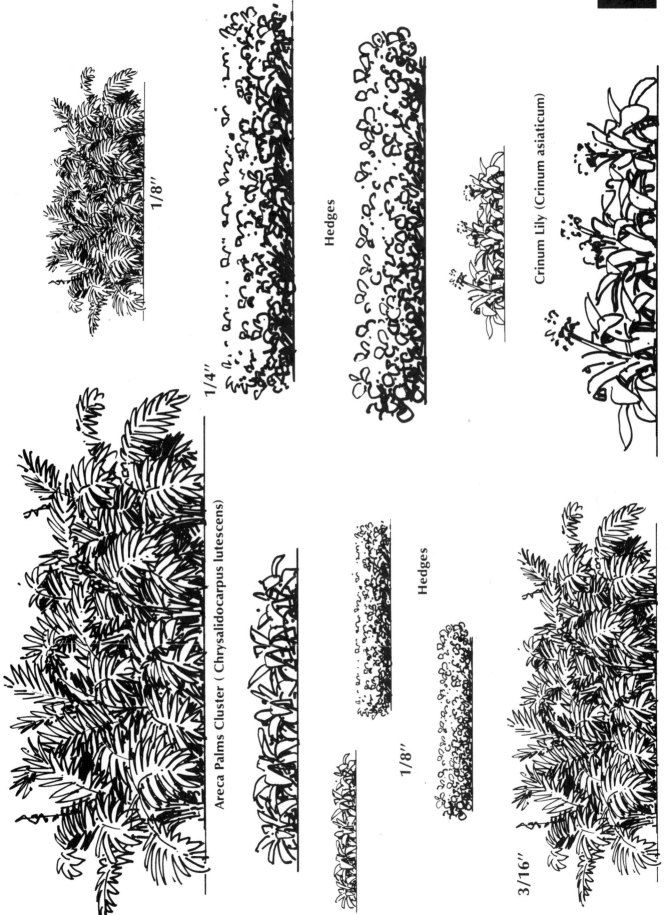

137

1/8"

1/4"

Hedges

Crinum Lily (Crinum asiaticum)

Areca Palms Cluster (Chrysalidocarpus lutescens)

Hedges

1/8"

3/16"

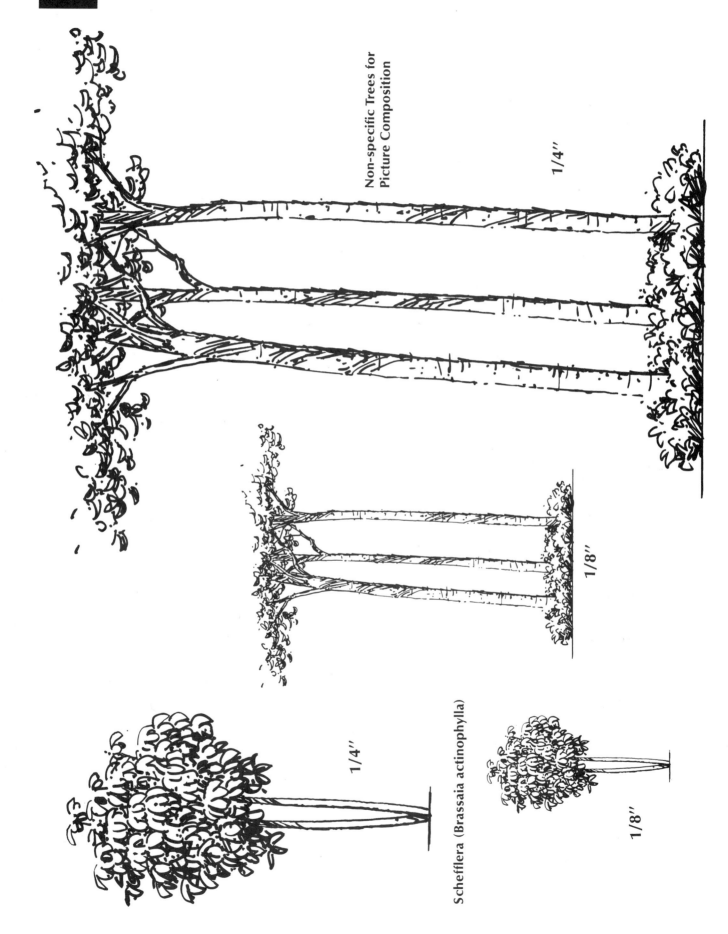

Non-specific Trees for
Picture Composition

1/4"

1/8"

Schefflera (Brassaia actinophylla)

1/4"

1/8"

1/4"

Pine Tree Cluster (Pinus clausa)

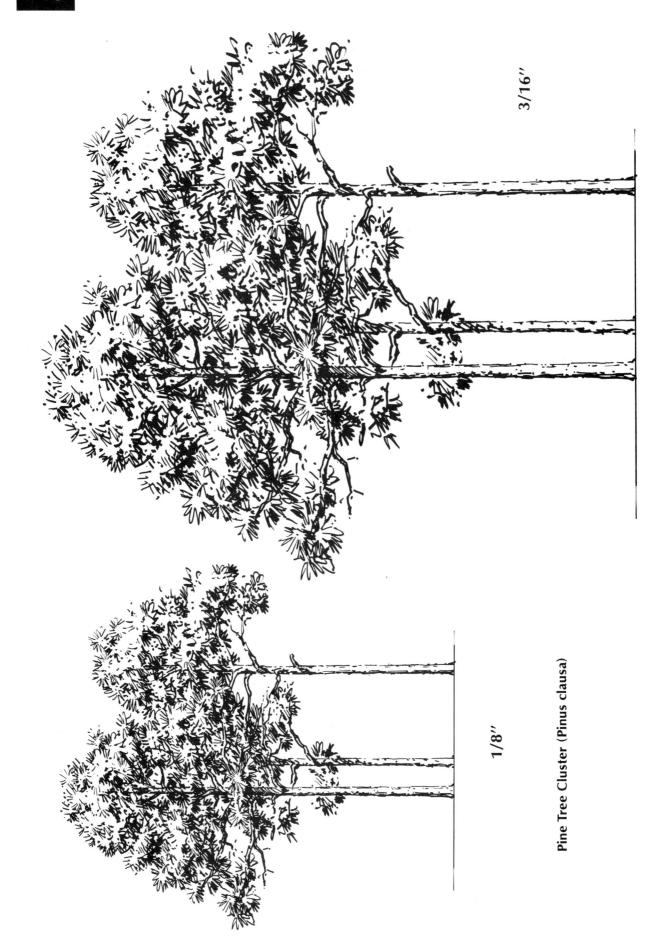

3/16"

1/8"

Pine Tree Cluster (Pinus clausa)

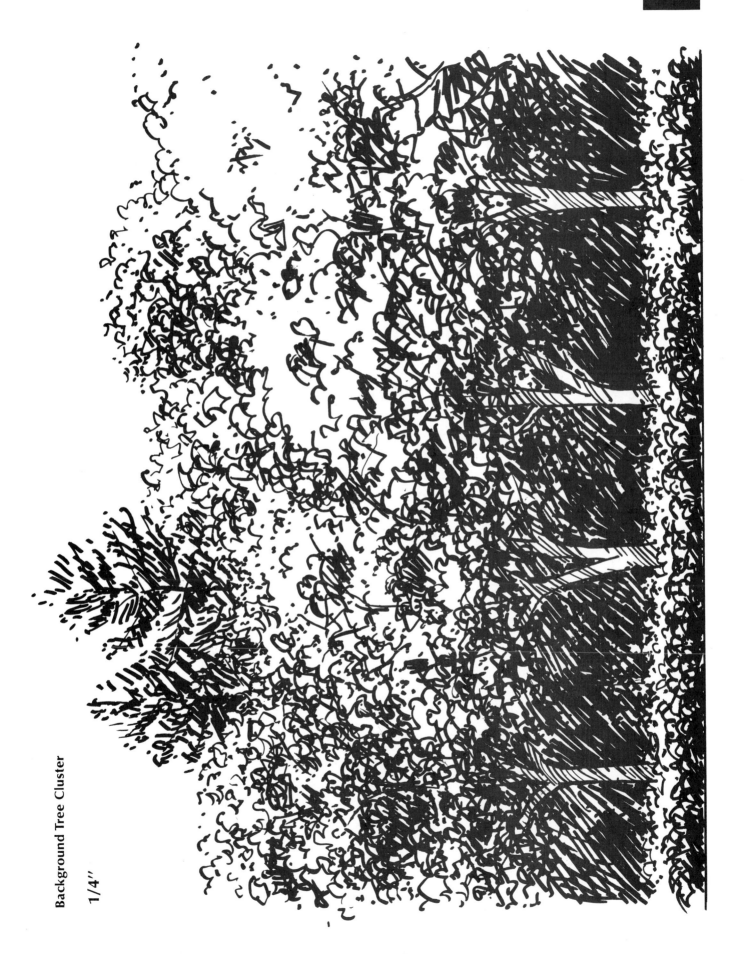

Background Tree Cluster

1/4"

Background Tree Cluster

3/16″

1/8″

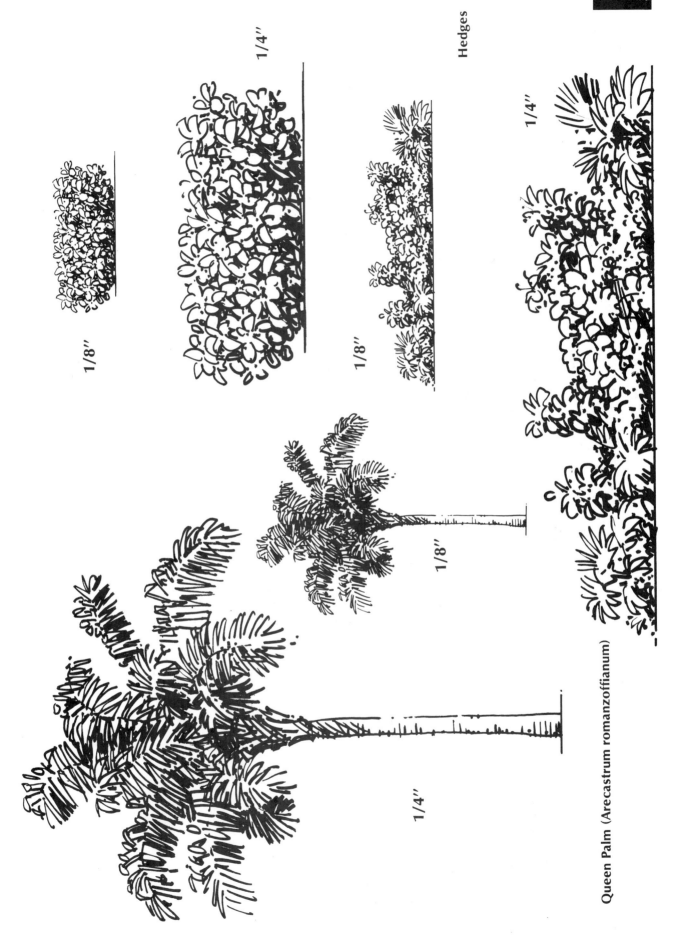

Hedges

1/4"

1/8"

1/4"

1/8"

1/4"

1/8"

1/4"

Queen Palm (Arecastrum romanzoffianum)

1/4"

1/8"

1/4"

1/8"

*N*o one really knows when the first person
put a plant in a pot and willed it to grow,
but drawings carved on the wall of an Egyptian
temple 3500 years ago depict people digging
up and potting frankincense trees for the
enjoyment of Queen Hatshepsut. Other early
renderings show urns, jardinieres, calabashes,
and woven baskets filled with soil and planted
with food crops and ornamental trees and vines.

Jim Wilson
Landscaping with Container Plants

Interior Foliage

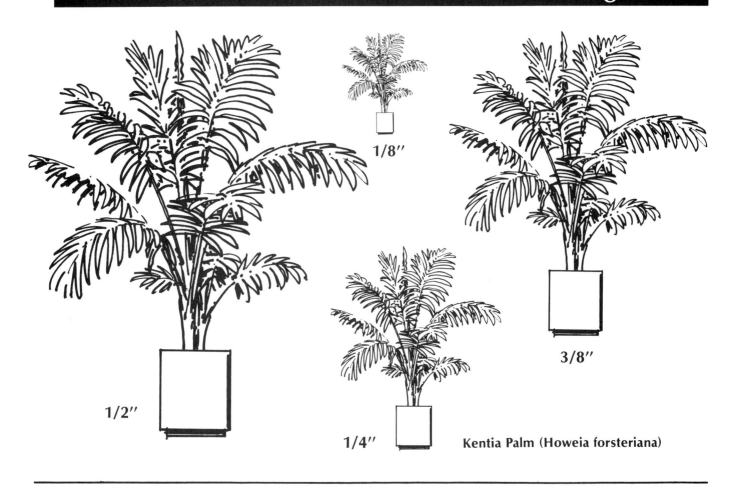

1/8″

1/2″

1/4″

3/8″

Kentia Palm (Howeia forsteriana)

Chamaedorea Palm (Chamaedorea erumpens)

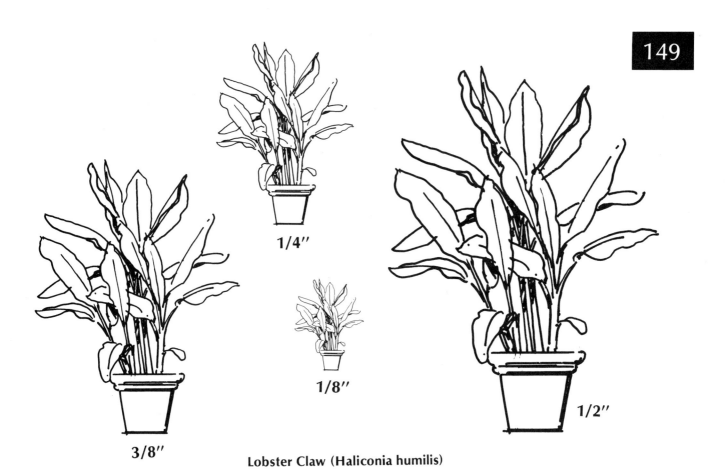

1/4″

1/8″

3/8″

1/2″

Lobster Claw (Haliconia humilis)

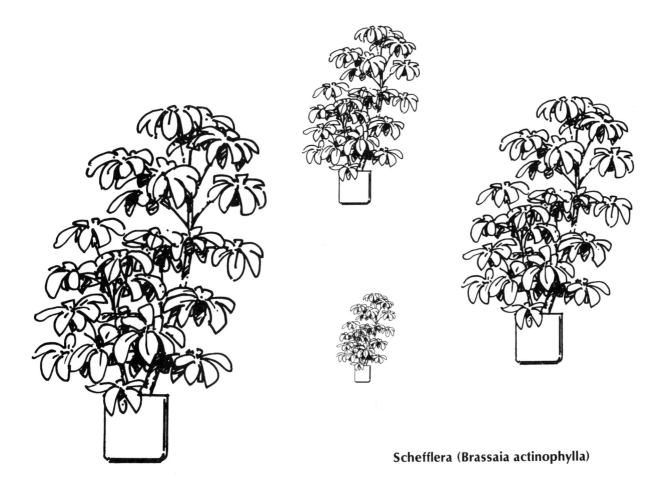

Schefflera (Brassaia actinophylla)

Banana (Musa paradisiaca)

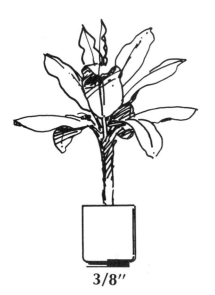

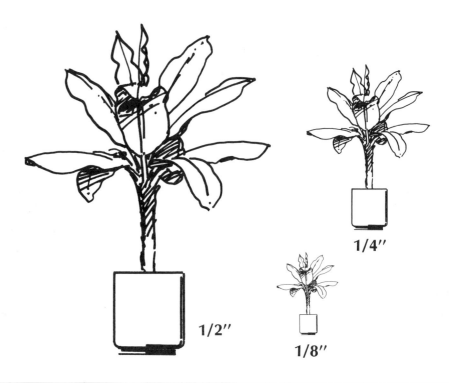

3/8"

1/2"

1/8"

1/4"

Corn Plant (Dracaena massangeana)

Coontie (Cycas floridana)

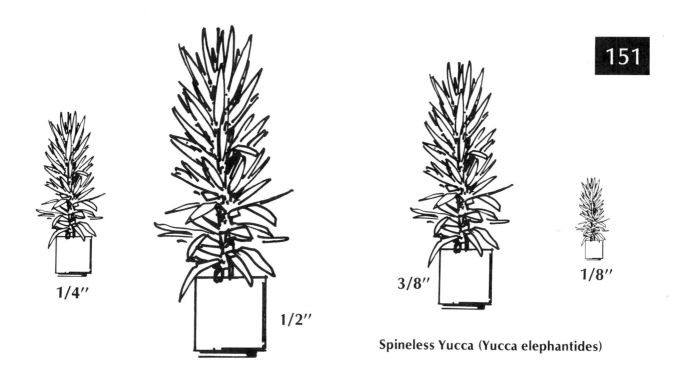

1/4"

1/2"

3/8"

1/8"

Spineless Yucca (Yucca elephantides)

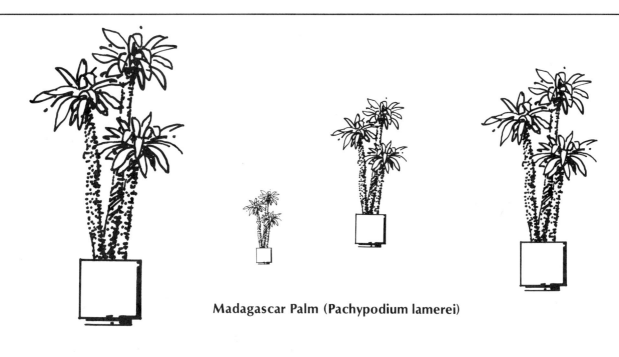

Madagascar Palm (Pachypodium lamerei)

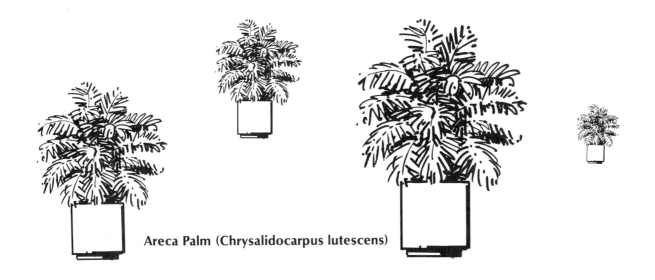

Areca Palm (Chrysalidocarpus lutescens)

1/8''

1/2''

3/8''

1/4''

Dracena (Dracaena marginata)

Screw Pine (Pandanus utilis)

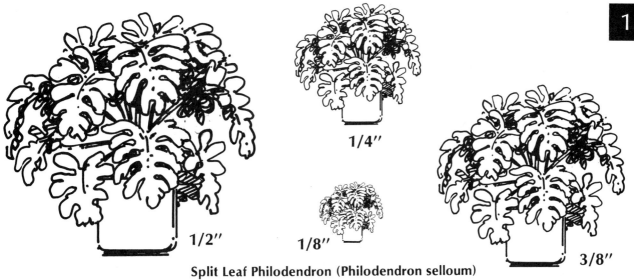

1/4"

1/8"

1/2"

3/8"

Split Leaf Philodendron (Philodendron selloum)

Hawaiian Schefflera (Brassaia arboricola)

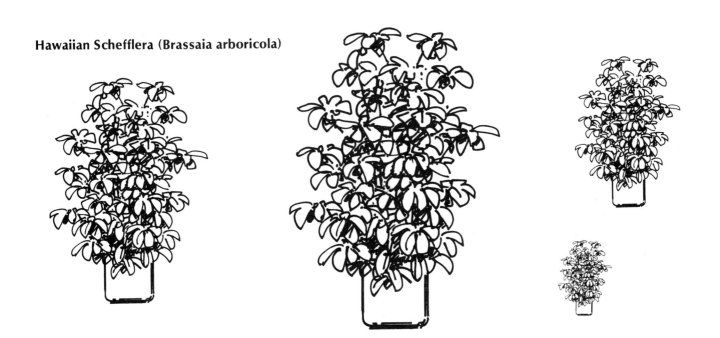

Pony Tail Palm (Beaucarnea recurvata)

Lady Palm (Rhapis excelsa)

3/8"

1/4"

1/2"

1/8"

Dumb Cane (Dieffenbachia exotica)

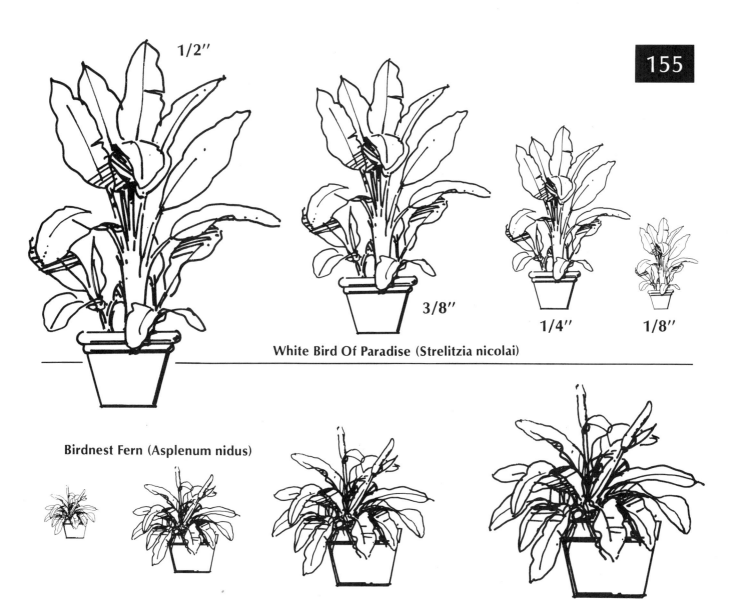

1/2″

3/8″

1/4″ 1/8″

White Bird Of Paradise (Strelitzia nicolai)

Birdnest Fern (Asplenum nidus)

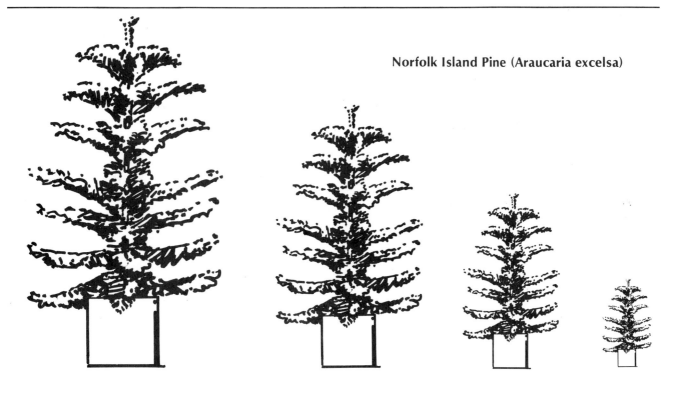

Norfolk Island Pine (Araucaria excelsa)

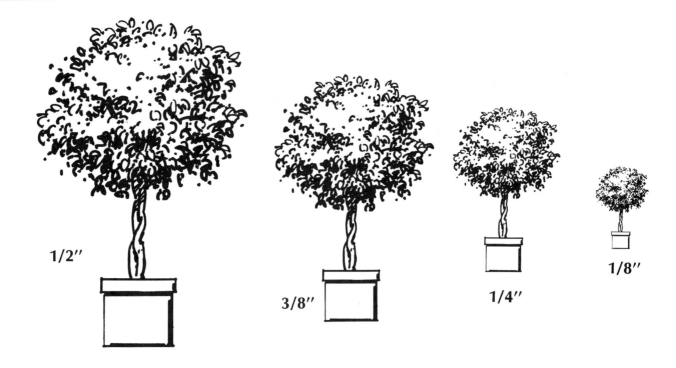

1/2″

3/8″

1/4″

1/8″

Weeping Fig - Braided (Ficus benjamina)

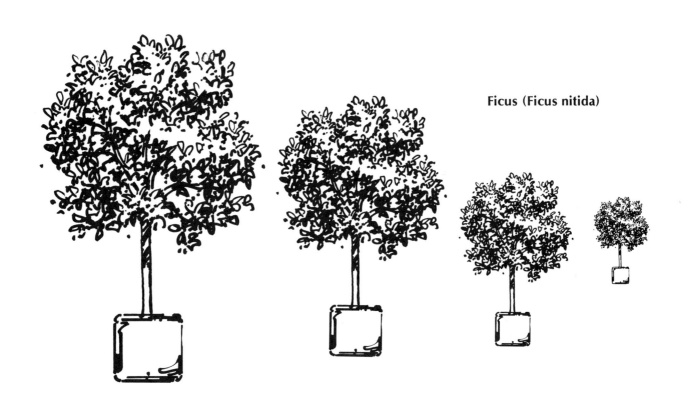

Ficus (Ficus nitida)

1/2"

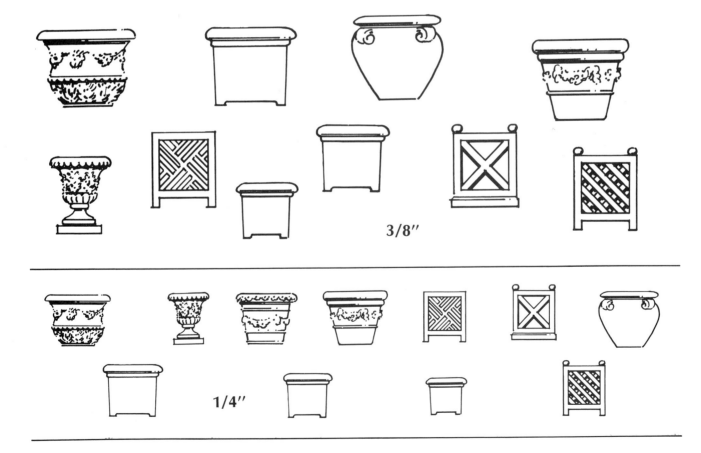

3/8"

1/4"

      1/8"

Index

Has SCALE ELEMENTS Helped You Create More Effective Presentation Elevations?

Then get

TRACING FILE

also by Richard M. McGarry, with over 1500 line drawings to use in your architectural and interior renderings.

Mail this coupon now to try out TRACING FILE

RISK-FREE for 15 days!

Most design presentations are done under a deadline, often a very difficult one, and Tracing File is designed to make fast work of finding appropriate entourage elements to add to your interior and architectural illustrations. It contains 280 pages of people in residential, commerical, and recreational situations, plus 17 different varieties of interior foliage plants. All pages are marked at the side with with a descriptive title, and cross-referenced to other pages of useful related material. Pages are also designed to be easily removed from the binding for adding to your rendering entourage file.

A chapter of concentric ellipses, in 23 different angles of inclination, is included for assistance in the sometimes difficult task of drawing circular shapes in perspective. Plus, a checklist provides a single-page digest of all the elements of good design presentation rendering, including both pointers for developing a rendering and critiquing your finished work.

ABOUT THE AUTHORS

"A design presentation's first job is to sell the project," according to Richard McGarry, "and the details are secondary to making a crisp, exciting picture that tells a story about the value of the concept." His firm, Richard M. McGarry Inc., creates renderings that sell the visions of architects, interior designers, real-estate developers, and advertising agencies.

Richard graduated with honors from Miami-Dade Community College, and continued his professional education at the University of Florida and the Art Center College of Design before opening his illustration practice in Miami, Florida, in 1975. He is a member of the Graphic Artists Guild, the Authors Guild, and the American Society of Architectural Perspectivists. His other books include *Tracing File for Interior and Architectural Rendering* and *Key West Sketchbook.*

Greg Madsen studied graphic design and illustration at the Art Institute of Ft. Lauderdale and was a free-lance illustrator for nine years before becoming a partner in Richard M. McGarry Inc. He specializes in marker design sketches for short deadlines, which is the subject of a book he is currently developing. Greg is a member of the Graphic Artists Guild and the American Society of Architectural Perspectivists.

NEED MORE HELP?

If you have any questions or comments about the material in this book, you can call the authors direct at (305) 757-5720. If you prefer, fax us your message at (305) 757-DRAW or write Richard M. McGarry Inc., 450 N.E. 52nd Terrace, Miami, Florida 33137.